The Gratitude Effec
Your Life One Than

BRENDA REBON

Visit our website for more inspiration, motivation, and self-improvement/
personal development info:

AchieveProgress.com

Table of Contents

Why I Wrote This Book...1

Why You Should Read This Book 3

The Power Of Gratitude: Understanding The Science And Benefits..........5

Cultivating a Grateful Mindset: Strategies for Developing Gratitude Awareness 9

Gratitude in Daily Life: Simple Practices to Foster Appreciation 14

Overcoming Gratitude Obstacles 19

The Grateful Heart: Strengthening Relationships Through Gratitude 24

Gratitude and Resilience: Navigating Life's Challenges with Grace and Appreciation 28

The Mind-Body Connection: How Gratitude Impacts Physical and Emotional Well-being.. 33

Gratitude at Work: Creating a Positive and Supportive Professional Environment 39

Parenting with Gratitude: Fostering Appreciation and Empathy in Children.. 44

The Art of Grateful Communication: Expressing Appreciation in Words and Actions 49

Gratitude and Spirituality: Exploring the Connection Between Gratitude and Inner Growth 54

A Grateful Worldview: Embracing the Beauty of Life's Imperfections 59

Gratitude in Difficult Times: Cultivating Resilience and Hope................ 64

Gratitude and Aging: Embracing the Golden Years with Grace and Appreciation 69

Living a Life of Gratitude: Embodying Gratitude in Daily Life 74

Conclusion... 81

A Personal Thank You 83

Other Books By Brenda Rebon 84

Frequently Asked Questions (FAQs) 88

Visit My Website for More Helpful Information 91

Copyright and Disclaimer

Why I Wrote This Book

I am often asked about my inspiration and motivation for writing this book. To answer this question, I want to share with you the reasons that fueled my passion for exploring and sharing the incredible power of gratitude.

1. **Personal transformation:** My own journey with gratitude began during a challenging period of my life when I was struggling with stress, anxiety, and feelings of overwhelm. Discovering and embracing the practice of gratitude transformed my outlook, emotional well-being, and relationships. This personal transformation ignited a deep desire to share the benefits of gratitude with others.

2. **The science of gratitude:** As I delved deeper into the world of gratitude, I was fascinated by the extensive research and scientific findings that demonstrated its numerous benefits. I felt compelled to share this knowledge, making the science of gratitude accessible and relatable to everyone, regardless of their background or familiarity with the topic.

3. **Creating lasting change:** My goal in writing this book was to provide readers with the tools and strategies needed to create a sustainable gratitude practice that could be integrated into their daily lives. By offering practical, actionable advice, I wanted to empower readers to make lasting changes and experience the profound benefits of gratitude for themselves.

4. **Strengthening relationships:** As I observed the positive impact of gratitude on my own relationships, I became passionate about exploring how gratitude could enhance our connections with others. I wanted to provide readers with insights and guidance on how to cultivate gratitude within their relationships, leading to deeper bonds and improved communication.

5. **Encouraging personal growth:** One of the most powerful aspects of gratitude is its ability to foster personal growth and transformation. Through writing this book, I sought to inspire readers to embrace gratitude as a catalyst for change, unlocking their full potential and helping them achieve their goals.

6. **Building a gratitude movement:** I truly believe that gratitude has the power to change not only individual lives but also the world around us. By writing this book, I hoped to contribute to a growing movement of individuals who recognize the value of gratitude and are committed to cultivating a life of appreciation and well-being.

7. **Leaving a legacy:** Lastly, I wrote this book as a way of sharing my gratitude journey and leaving a lasting impact on the lives of others. My hope is that "The Gratitude Mindset: Unlocking the Power of Thankfulness in Your Life" serves as a source of inspiration and guidance for those seeking to create a more fulfilling, joyful, and connected life.

My journey as an author was driven by the transformative power of gratitude that I experienced in my own life. I hope that by sharing my knowledge, insights, and personal experiences, this book will inspire and empower you to embrace gratitude and unlock its incredible potential in your life.

Warmest regards,
Brenda Rebon

Why You Should Read This Book

In today's fast-paced and often stressful world, it can be all too easy to lose sight of the things that truly matter. Amid the chaos and distractions, finding a sense of appreciation and contentment can seem like a daunting task. However, cultivating gratitude has been scientifically proven to significantly improve our overall well-being, happiness, and relationships. This is an essential guide for anyone seeking to harness the benefits of gratitude and create a more fulfilling life.

Here are some compelling reasons why you should read this book:

1. **Comprehensive and research-based:** This book covers the science, practice, and impact of gratitude, providing a thorough understanding of how gratitude works and why it is so beneficial. You will gain insights into the latest research on gratitude and its effects on the brain, psychological well-being, physical health, and relationships.

2. **Practical and actionable advice:** The book offers a wealth of strategies and techniques for cultivating gratitude in various aspects of your life. From simple daily practices to more in-depth techniques, you will learn how to develop and maintain a sustainable gratitude practice that is tailored to your unique needs and preferences.

3. **Enhance your emotional well-being:** Cultivating gratitude has been proven to increase happiness, life satisfaction, and resilience in the face of adversity. This book will teach you how to use gratitude practices to boost your emotional well-being, reduce stress, and develop a more positive outlook on life.

4. **Improve your relationships:** Gratitude has a powerful impact on our connections with others, fostering deeper bonds, increased empathy, and improved communication. By learning how to express and cultivate gratitude in your relationships, you can enhance your

personal and professional connections and create more meaningful interactions with those around you.

5. **Support your physical health:** Gratitude has been linked to numerous physical health benefits, including improved sleep, increased immunity, and better pain management. This book will explore the mind-body connection and offer practical tips for harnessing the power of gratitude to support your overall health and well-being.

6. **Encourage personal growth:** Gratitude practices can serve as a catalyst for change, unlocking your full potential and helping you achieve your goals. This book offers insights and strategies for using gratitude to foster creativity, problem-solving, and transformation.

7. **Join a growing community:** By reading this book, you will become part of a growing community of individuals who recognize the value of gratitude and are committed to cultivating a life of appreciation and well-being.

This is more than just a book—it's an invitation to embark on a life-changing journey of self-discovery, personal growth, and profound appreciation. Start your gratitude journey today and experience the transformative power of thankfulness.

Warmest regards,

Brenda Rebon

The Power Of Gratitude: Understanding The Science And Benefits

"Gratitude is not only the greatest of virtues but the parent of all others." - Cicero

The Science Behind Gratitude: Neurological and Psychological Perspectives

Understanding the Neurobiology of Gratitude: Gratitude is more than just a feel-good emotion; it has a deep-seated connection with our brain's neurological processes. When we express gratitude, our brain releases dopamine and serotonin, the two crucial neurotransmitters responsible for our emotions. They enhance our mood, making us feel 'happier' from within.

Gratitude and the Brain's Reward System: The human brain's reward system is significantly influenced by feelings of gratitude. When we express or receive gratitude, our brain's reward pathways activate, releasing a surge of feel-good chemicals and generating a sense of pleasure.

The Role of Gratitude in Positive Psychology: Positive psychology studies the aspects that make life most worth living, and gratitude sits at the heart of it. By focusing on gratitude, we can foster optimism, enhance well-being, and increase life satisfaction.

Gratitude and the Release of "Feel Good" Hormones: Gratitude aids in the release of hormones such as dopamine and serotonin, which boost our mood. These chemicals help us maintain a positive outlook, even when we face challenges or adversity.

How Gratitude Affects Brain Structure Over Time: Gratitude can have long-lasting effects on the brain. Regular practice of gratitude can change our brain's neural structures, enhance the production of dopamine, and encourage the brain to adopt positivity as a default state.

The Physical Benefits of Gratitude: Health and Wellness Impacts

Gratitude and Improved Sleep Quality: Gratitude can significantly improve sleep quality. Keeping a gratitude journal and writing in it before bedtime helps individuals feel more relaxed and obtain more restful sleep.

The Connection Between Gratitude and Immune System Health: Gratitude can help boost the immune system. Positive emotions, including gratitude, have been associated with better immune function, especially in stress-related contexts.

Gratitude and its Impact on Pain Levels: Gratitude can also help manage pain levels. People who regularly practice gratitude have been found to experience less pain and are more likely to take care of their health.

The Role of Gratitude in Stress Reduction: Gratitude has been linked to stress reduction. By focusing on positive experiences and blessings, individuals can reframe negative or stressful situations, leading to lower stress levels.

Gratitude and Its Role in Overall Longevity: While direct research on gratitude and longevity is limited, studies suggest that a positive attitude, including regular gratitude practice, can impact longevity. A consistent state of gratitude can lead to a healthier heart, improved immune function, and better physical health - all contributing factors to a longer life.

Emotional Well-being: How Gratitude Affects Happiness and Life Satisfaction

Gratitude: A Key to Happiness: Gratitude plays a crucial role in enhancing happiness. It shifts our focus from what's lacking in our lives to the abundance that's already present, leading to a greater sense of happiness.

How Gratitude Boosts Mood and Reduces Depression: Gratitude practices, like journaling or mental countdowns of things you're grateful for, can help in reducing feelings of depression and boosting mood. By focusing on positive experiences, people can shift their mindset towards positivity.

The Correlation Between Gratitude and Life Satisfaction: Gratitude is strongly correlated with life satisfaction. By appreciating what we have, we can feel more content with our current situation, improving our overall satisfaction with life.

The Role of Gratitude in Resilience: Resilience, or our ability to bounce back from adversity, can be significantly boosted by gratitude. Recognizing and appreciating the good in life helps us maintain a positive perspective during tough times, thereby enhancing our resilience.

Cultivating Positive Emotions Through Gratitude: Gratitude encourages the cultivation of positive emotions, like joy and contentment, by shifting our focus away from negative aspects and towards what enriches our lives. This shift can lead to a more optimistic outlook and greater emotional well-being.

Gratitude and Relationships: Strengthening Connections with Others

The Role of Gratitude in Romantic Relationships: Gratitude can strengthen romantic relationships. Appreciating your partner's positive attributes and actions can enhance relationship satisfaction, deepen emotional connections, and improve communication.

How Gratitude Strengthens Friendships: Gratitude can also enhance friendships. Expressing appreciation for friends can build stronger connections, encourage mutual support, and create a positive feedback loop of gratitude and appreciation.

Gratitude and Family Relationships: Gratitude practices within families can foster stronger bonds, mutual respect, and positive communication. Regular expressions of gratitude can make family members feel valued and appreciated.

Gratitude in Professional Relationships: In the workplace, gratitude can build stronger teams, enhance job satisfaction, and improve overall productivity. Employees who feel appreciated are more motivated and committed.

Expressing Gratitude to Strengthen Social Bonds: Expressing gratitude can also strengthen broader social bonds. By recognizing the contributions of others, we can create a more connected, supportive, and positive community.

The Broader Implications of Gratitude: Workplace, Community, and Global Effects

The Impact of Gratitude in the Workplace: Gratitude in the workplace can lead to improved employee morale, increased productivity, and a more positive work environment. It can also decrease stress and job dissatisfaction.

Gratitude and Community Building: Gratitude can play a significant role in building stronger communities. Expressing gratitude within a community can foster mutual support, enhance social connections, and contribute to a more positive and cooperative environment.

The Role of Gratitude in Global Peace and Understanding: At a global level, gratitude can foster peace and understanding. Recognizing and appreciating cultural diversity, shared humanity, and global interdependence can encourage peacebuilding and international cooperation.

How Gratitude Can Foster a More Positive Society: A society in which gratitude is widely practiced can be more positive and harmonious. Such societies may experience reduced conflict, increased mutual respect, and a greater focus on collective well-being.

Gratitude and its Impact on Environmental Consciousness: Gratitude towards nature can enhance environmental consciousness. Appreciating the natural world can lead to more sustainable behaviors and greater commitment to environmental conservation.

Cultivating a Grateful Mindset: Strategies for Developing Gratitude Awareness

R*egularly expressing gratitude rewires the brain to focus more on positive aspects of life.*

The Role of Mindfulness in Cultivating Gratitude

Mindfulness as a Pathway to Gratitude: Mindfulness, or the practice of being fully present and engaged in the current moment, is a powerful pathway to gratitude. By focusing on the here and now, we become more attuned to the positive aspects of our lives, fostering a sense of gratitude.

Mindful Meditation for Enhancing Gratitude: Mindful meditation can enhance feelings of gratitude. During meditation, we can focus on things we appreciate, fostering a deeper sense of gratitude and well-being.

Present Moment Awareness and Gratitude: Present moment awareness, a key element of mindfulness, is closely linked to gratitude. By focusing on the present, we can shift our attention away from past regrets and future anxieties, allowing us to appreciate and be grateful for the present moment.

Mindfulness Exercises to Cultivate Gratitude: Mindfulness exercises such as mindful eating, mindful walking, or simply focusing on your breath can help cultivate gratitude. These practices make us more aware of our experiences, encouraging appreciation for the simple things in life.

The Interplay Between Mindfulness and Gratitude in Emotional Well-being: Mindfulness and gratitude together play a significant role in emotional well-being. Both practices encourage a focus on the positive aspects of life, fostering optimism, contentment, and overall happiness.

Reframing Negative Thoughts: Shifting Perspectives to Find Gratitude

Cognitive Reframing Techniques for Gratitude: Cognitive reframing is a psychological technique that involves identifying and then changing the way situations, experiences, or thoughts are viewed. Reframing can help us find gratitude even in challenging situations.

The Role of Gratitude in Overcoming Negative Thinking: Gratitude can play a significant role in overcoming negative thinking. By focusing on things, we are grateful for, we can shift our mindset from negativity and dissatisfaction to positivity and appreciation.

How to Practice Gratitude in Difficult Times: Practicing gratitude in difficult times can be challenging, but it is possible and beneficial. By finding small things to be thankful for, we can cultivate a sense of hope and positivity that can help us navigate through adversity.

The Power of Positivity: Gratitude in the Face of Adversity: Gratitude can be a powerful tool in the face of adversity. By focusing on what we can be thankful for, we can foster a positive outlook that can help us overcome challenges and foster resilience.

Transforming Pessimism into Optimism Through Gratitude: Gratitude can transform a pessimistic mindset into a more optimistic one. By recognizing and appreciating the good in our lives, we can shift our focus away from negatives, fostering a more positive and optimistic outlook.

Gratitude Triggers: Identifying and Utilizing Daily Reminders

Utilizing Technology to Trigger Gratitude Reminders: In our digital age, technology can serve as a potent tool for triggering gratitude reminders. Smartphone apps, digital calendars, or even simple alarm reminders can be programmed to prompt regular moments of gratitude reflection.

Creating Personal Rituals as Gratitude Triggers: Creating personal rituals can be an effective way to cultivate gratitude. These could include practices like writing in a gratitude journal each night, sharing something you're grateful for at mealtimes, or taking a daily gratitude walk.

Building a Gratitude Routine: Integrating Practices into Your Everyday Life

Developing a Daily Gratitude Journaling Routine: Gratitude journaling is a common and effective practice for cultivating gratitude. By setting aside time each day to write down things we're grateful for, we can foster a more positive mindset and increase our overall sense of well-being.

Incorporating Gratitude into Morning and Evening Routines: Incorporating gratitude practices into our morning and evening routines can help start and end our day on a positive note. This could be as simple as thinking of three things we're grateful for each morning and night.

Gratitude Practices for Mealtimes: Mealtimes offer an excellent opportunity for gratitude practices. This could involve expressing gratitude for the food, the company, or simply the time to relax and enjoy the meal.

Cultivating Gratitude Through Regular Mindfulness Practices: Regular mindfulness practices, such as meditation or yoga, can help cultivate gratitude. These practices encourage us to slow down, be present, and appreciate the richness of our experiences.

How to Make Gratitude a Habit: Making gratitude a habit involves regular and consistent practice. Like any habit, the key is to start small, be consistent, and gradually gratitude will become a natural and integral part of your daily life.

Developing Gratitude Habits: Tips for Long-lasting Change

The Science of Habit Formation and Its Application to Gratitude: Understanding the science of habit formation can help in developing lasting gratitude habits. By leveraging the habit loop of cue, routine, and reward, we can create and maintain a regular practice of gratitude.

Practical Strategies for Cultivating Gratitude Habits: Practical strategies for cultivating gratitude habits might include setting clear intentions, scheduling regular gratitude time, using reminders or triggers, and practicing patience and persistence.

Overcoming Obstacles in Developing Gratitude Habits: Obstacles to developing gratitude habits might include forgetfulness, lack of time, or a negative mindset. These can be overcome by setting realistic expectations, making gratitude practices simple and enjoyable, and remembering the benefits of gratitude.

Reinforcing and Rewarding Gratitude Habits: Reinforcing and rewarding gratitude habits can help them stick. This could involve rewarding yourself with a treat, a break, or simply a moment of recognition when you stick to your gratitude practice.

Tracking Progress in Gratitude Habit Formation: Tracking progress can be a powerful motivator in the formation of gratitude habits. This could involve keeping a record of your daily gratitude entries, noting changes in your mood or outlook, or simply marking off each successful day on a calendar.

Understanding Gratitude Stacking: What It Is and Why It Matters

Gratitude Stacking is a concept that involves acknowledging and appreciating multiple things in your life at once, essentially "stacking" your gratefulness. This practice goes beyond the basic gratitude journaling or reflection by asking you to acknowledge multiple positive elements, experiences, or individuals that you're thankful for in a continuous, flowing thought process. The idea behind gratitude stacking is that by layering one thankful thought on top of another, you can create a more profound sense of gratitude and positive emotion. This practice matters as it encourages a deeper, more comprehensive exploration of positivity, thus fostering a higher overall sense of well-being and happiness.

The Benefits of Gratitude Stacking: How It Enhances Your Gratitude Practice

Gratitude Stacking enhances your gratitude practice by amplifying the emotional and cognitive benefits associated with gratitude. By reflecting on multiple points of gratitude at once, you engage your brain more fully in the process, deepening your emotional response and increasing your sense of well-being. This practice can lead to enhanced mood, improved outlook on life, better stress management, and increased resilience. It also allows you to recognize the interconnectedness of the positive elements in your life, fostering a more holistic sense of appreciation.

The Neuroscience of Gratitude Stacking: The Cumulative Impact on the Brain

Neuroscientific research suggests that practicing gratitude can lead to changes in various brain regions, including those involved in emotion regulation, self-referential processing, and reward. Gratitude stacking may have a cumulative effect on the brain, enhancing these changes due to the continuous, concentrated focus on positive experiences. This repetitive focus on positive experiences can reinforce neural pathways associated with positive emotions and thoughts, potentially leading to long-term changes in brain function and structure, enhancing emotional well-being, and promoting a positive outlook.

Integrating Gratitude Stacking into Your Daily Routine

Gratitude stacking can be integrated into your daily routine in various ways. One effective method is to dedicate a few minutes each day, perhaps in the morning or before bed, to think about multiple things you're grateful for and reflect on how they interconnect. This could be done through silent reflection, journaling, or even while performing daily tasks like showering or commuting. The key is to consciously focus on a series of positive elements in your life, allowing your mind to move seamlessly from one point of gratitude to the next.

Gratitude Stacking and Personal Growth: Developing Emotional Resilience and Well-being

Gratitude stacking can play a significant role in personal growth by fostering emotional resilience and well-being. By consistently focusing on the positive aspects of your life and recognizing their interconnectedness, you can develop a more optimistic outlook, improve your ability to cope with stress and adversity, and enhance your overall emotional well-being. This practice can help you cultivate a stronger sense of self-worth, improve your relationships, and promote a greater appreciation for life, all of which contribute to personal growth and development.

Gratitude in Daily Life: Simple Practices to Foster Appreciation

"The root of joy is gratefulness." - David Steindl-Rast*

The Gratitude Journal: Recording and Reflecting on Appreciation

Starting a Gratitude Journal: The act of writing down what you are thankful for in a gratitude journal serves as a reminder of the good things in life. It also helps in shifting our focus from negative aspects to the positive ones, thereby fostering a positive outlook on life. By consistently writing in a gratitude journal, you train your brain to notice the good things, thus rewiring it towards positivity.

The Role of Reflection in Gratitude Journaling: Reflection is a vital aspect of gratitude journaling. It helps you to dig deeper into your feelings and understand why you are grateful for certain things or people. This understanding can enhance the quality of your gratitude and make it more meaningful.

How to Maintain a Gratitude Journal: Consistency is key in gratitude journaling. It is not the number of things you list that matters but the regularity of the practice. Whether you choose to write in your journal daily, weekly, or at another interval, what's important is that you make it a regular practice.

The Benefits of Gratitude Journaling: Gratitude journaling has been linked to several psychological benefits including increased happiness, reduced stress levels, and improved sleep. It can also improve physical health, reduce symptoms of illness, and lead to healthier behaviors.

Gratitude Journaling Techniques: There are several techniques for gratitude journaling. Some people prefer to write in the morning to start their day on a positive note, while others prefer to write before bed to end their day with positivity. Additionally, some people prefer to write freely about their feelings of gratitude, while others prefer to list what they are grateful for.

Gratitude Meditation: Cultivating Thankfulness Through Mindful Practices

The Basics of Gratitude Meditation: Gratitude meditation is a type of meditation where you focus on the things, people, or experiences you are grateful for. It involves quieting the mind and focusing on feelings of gratitude, which can create a sense of calm and positivity.

How to Practice Gratitude Meditation: To practice gratitude meditation, find a quiet space where you can focus on your thoughts. Begin by taking a few deep breaths to calm your mind. Then, bring to mind something or someone you are grateful for. Spend a few moments focusing on the feelings of gratitude that arise.

The Benefits of Gratitude Meditation: Gratitude meditation has been shown to reduce stress, improve emotional well-being, and increase mindfulness. It can also lead to improved physical health, including better sleep, fewer symptoms of illness, and increased happiness.

Integrating Gratitude Meditation into Your Daily Routine: Gratitude meditation can be easily integrated into your daily routine. You can practice it in the morning to start your day with a positive mindset, or in the evening to reflect on the positive aspects of your day.

Gratitude Meditation Techniques: There are several techniques for practicing gratitude meditation. Some people prefer to focus on a specific object of gratitude, while others prefer to let their mind wander and see what arises. Additionally, some people find it helpful to use guided meditation.

Expressing Gratitude: Verbal and Non-verbal Ways to Show Appreciation

The Power of Saying Thank You: The simple act of saying "thank you" can have profound effects. It can make people feel valued and appreciated, and it can strengthen relationships. Additionally, expressing gratitude can improve your own well-being, as it can shift your focus from what's going wrong to what's going right.

The Role of Non-Verbal Expressions of Gratitude: Non-verbal expressions of gratitude such as a warm smile, a hug, or a thoughtful gesture can often convey more than words. These expressions can show sincerity and deepen the connection between individuals.

How to Incorporate Gratitude Expressions in Daily Life: Incorporating expressions of gratitude into daily life can be as simple as regularly saying "thank you", writing thank-you notes, or showing appreciation through acts of kindness. These practices can make gratitude a habit and enhance overall well-being.

The Impact of Expressing Gratitude on Relationships: Expressing gratitude can have a significant positive impact on relationships. It can increase relationship satisfaction, strengthen bonds, and promote reciprocal kindness. It also fosters a positive environment where appreciation is valued and expressed freely.

Gratitude Expression Techniques: There are many ways to express gratitude. Some people prefer verbal expressions, while others prefer written notes. Other techniques include acts of service, spending quality time, and giving gifts. These techniques align with the five love languages outlined by Dr. Gary Chapman, suggesting that our preferred ways of expressing gratitude may be linked to our love languages.

Gratitude Prompts: Guided Practices for Cultivating Appreciation

The Role of Gratitude Prompts: Gratitude prompts are questions or statements designed to help individuals identify things they're grateful for. They can be particularly helpful for those who struggle to think of things to write in a gratitude journal or focus on during a gratitude meditation.

Using Gratitude Prompts in a Journal: Gratitude prompts can be used in a gratitude journal to guide reflections on gratitude. They can help to deepen the practice by encouraging individuals to think more deeply and specifically about what they're grateful for.

Gratitude Prompts for Meditation: Gratitude prompts can also be used in meditation. They can be used to guide the focus towards specific areas of life or experiences for which to feel grateful.

Benefits of Using Gratitude Prompts: Using gratitude prompts can make the practice of cultivating gratitude more engaging and meaningful. It can also improve the ability to recognize and appreciate the good things in life.

Examples of Gratitude Prompts: There are many different gratitude prompts that can be used, depending on personal preferences and areas of life to focus on. Some examples include: "What is something you're grateful for in your home?" "Who is someone who made your day better?" "What is a personal accomplishment you're proud of?"

Gratitude Affirmations: Positive Statements for Fostering Thankfulness

Understanding Gratitude Affirmations: Gratitude affirmations are positive statements that help foster a sense of thankfulness. They are typically present-tense statements about being grateful for something in life, such as "I am grateful for my health" or "I appreciate the love in my life".

How to Use Gratitude Affirmations: Gratitude affirmations can be used in various ways. They can be written in a gratitude journal, repeated during meditation, or said out loud at certain times of the day. They can also be used as mantras during challenging times to foster positivity.

The Benefits of Gratitude Affirmations: Gratitude affirmations can help to cultivate a positive mindset, reduce stress, and improve overall well-being. By focusing on positive statements of gratitude, individuals can shift their focus from negative thoughts and foster a greater sense of appreciation for their life.

Integrating Gratitude Affirmations into Your Daily Routine: Gratitude affirmations can be easily integrated into a daily routine. They can be said upon waking up, before going to bed, or during moments of stress. Over time, this practice can help train the mind to focus more on the positive aspects of life, even in the face of adversity.

Creating Your Own Gratitude Affirmations: The process of creating your own gratitude affirmations involves identifying the things in your life that you feel most grateful for. These can be broad aspects, such as health or family, or they can be specific things, such as a recent accomplishment or a particular relationship. Once identified, these aspects can be formulated into positive present-tense statements that resonate with you.

Overcoming Gratitude Obstacles

F*act: It is estimated that only 20% of Americans rate gratitude as a positive, constructive emotion, yet its transformative power is unparalleled.*

Debunking Gratitude Myths: Misconceptions and Misunderstandings

Myth 1: Gratitude is Only for Certain Times: Many people believe that gratitude is something that should only be expressed during times of joy or when receiving a gift. However, research has shown that expressing gratitude even during difficult times can lead to increased resilience and a better ability to cope with stress.

Myth 2: Expressing Gratitude is a Sign of Weakness: Some cultures and societies may view the expression of gratitude as a sign of submission or weakness. This, however, is a misconception. Expressing gratitude is actually a sign of strength and maturity and fosters better social relationships and mental health.

Myth 3: Gratitude is About Ignoring Negative Emotions: Gratitude is not about denying or ignoring negative emotions. It's about acknowledging the good things in life without denying the existence of the bad. It's a balanced approach to life.

Myth 4: Gratitude is a Religious Practice: While many religions do encourage the practice of gratitude, it is not solely a religious concept. Gratitude is a universal human emotion that can be experienced and expressed by anyone, regardless of religious affiliation.

Myth 5: Gratitude Practices Take a Lot of Time: Many people believe that implementing gratitude practices into their daily lives will be time-consuming.

However, simple practices like keeping a gratitude journal or taking a moment each day to reflect on what you're grateful for can be done in just a few minutes and can have substantial benefits.

Gratitude in Difficult Times: Finding Appreciation Amidst Challenges

The Role of Gratitude in Difficult Times: Gratitude can play a pivotal role during challenging periods in our lives. It can help us to see the positive aspects of our situation and can be a powerful tool for resilience. Research indicates that people who regularly practice gratitude can better handle stress and adversity.

Techniques for Practicing Gratitude in Difficult Times: Techniques can include writing in a gratitude journal, practicing mindfulness, or even expressing gratitude to others. These methods can help us to shift our focus from the negative aspects of our situation to the positive, thereby promoting a more optimistic outlook.

The Impact of Gratitude on Mental Health During Difficult Times: By helping us to focus on the positive, gratitude can aid in reducing feelings of anxiety and depression. It has been shown to increase happiness and well-being, even in the face of significant challenges.

Gratitude and Resilience: Gratitude can also help to build resilience, enabling us to bounce back from adversity more quickly. It can provide us with a greater sense of self-worth and control over our lives, both of which are crucial for resilience.

The Challenges of Practicing Gratitude in Difficult Times: Despite its benefits, practicing gratitude during difficult times can be challenging. It requires a deliberate shift in mindset and a commitment to focusing on the positive, even when faced with adversity.

The Balance of Gratitude: Avoiding Toxic Positivity and Spiritual Bypassing

Understanding Toxic Positivity and Spiritual Bypassing: Toxic positivity refers to the overgeneralization of a happy, optimistic state that results in the denial, minimization, and invalidation of authentic human emotional experience. Spiritual bypassing is a related concept where spirituality is used to sidestep or avoid confronting emotional wounds, unfinished business, and unmet developmental needs.

The Importance of Balance in Gratitude Practice: While gratitude can improve mental health and overall well-being, it's essential to balance it with the acceptance and acknowledgment of painful emotions. Ignoring or suppressing negative feelings can lead to harmful consequences.

Navigating Difficult Emotions with Gratitude: Gratitude isn't about ignoring life's challenges or pain; it's about finding a way to appreciate the good in spite of these difficulties. Mindful gratitude can help us navigate through negative emotions and find solace in the lessons and strengths gained through these experiences.

Avoiding Gratitude Extremes: A healthy gratitude practice involves recognizing and accepting all emotions without judgement, including negative ones. By avoiding the extremes of toxic positivity and spiritual bypassing, gratitude can be a supportive tool for holistic growth.

Integrating Negative Emotions into Gratitude Practice: Negative emotions can be integrated into a gratitude practice by acknowledging them, understanding their source, and gleaning lessons from them. This integration can enhance emotional intelligence and resilience.

Overcoming Gratitude Resistance: Addressing Inner Barriers

Identifying Inner Barriers to Gratitude: Inner barriers to gratitude may include past trauma, fear of vulnerability, or a pattern of negative thinking. Understanding these barriers is the first step to overcoming them and fully embracing a gratitude practice.

Techniques for Overcoming Gratitude Resistance: Techniques to overcome gratitude resistance can include cognitive behavioral therapy, mindfulness practices, journaling, and seeking professional help. Each method serves to challenge and alter ingrained patterns of negative thinking.

The Role of Self-Compassion in Overcoming Gratitude Resistance: Self-compassion involves being open to and moved by one's own suffering, experiencing feelings of caring and kindness toward oneself, and not avoiding or disconnecting from one's painful experiences. Self-compassion can play a vital role in overcoming resistance to gratitude, as it encourages acceptance and love for oneself, even in the face of personal flaws or mistakes.

Gratitude and Emotional Resilience: Gratitude can enhance emotional resilience by promoting positive emotions even in the face of adversity. By focusing on the good, individuals can bounce back from negative experiences more effectively and maintain a positive outlook.

Long-term Strategies for Overcoming Gratitude Resistance: Building long-term strategies such as maintaining a regular gratitude practice, pursuing personal growth, fostering healthy relationships, and practicing mindfulness can help overcome gratitude resistance and cultivate a more appreciative outlook on life.

Nurturing a Growth Mindset: Embracing the Process of Developing Gratitude

The Concept of Growth Mindset: A growth mindset, as conceptualized by psychologist Carol Dweck, is the belief that one's abilities and intelligence can be developed through dedication and hard work. This perspective creates a love of learning, a resilience to setbacks, and an openness to self-improvement that are fundamental for achieving success.

Growth Mindset and Gratitude: Cultivating a growth mindset can enhance one's gratitude practice. By viewing gratitude not as a fixed trait but as a skill to be developed, individuals can learn to appreciate their progress, embrace challenges, and remain persistent in their efforts to cultivate thankfulness.

Strategies for Developing a Growth Mindset: Strategies for developing a growth mindset include recognizing and reframing negative self-talk, embracing challenges as opportunities for growth, and learning to view effort as a path to mastery. These practices can foster a more positive and resilient attitude towards personal development and progress.

The Role of Mindfulness in Nurturing a Growth Mindset: Mindfulness, the practice of focusing one's awareness on the present moment, can support the cultivation of a growth mindset. By non-judgmentally acknowledging thoughts and emotions, individuals can better recognize opportunities for growth and change.

The Long-Term Benefits of a Growth Mindset: Over time, a growth mindset can lead to higher levels of self-efficacy, resilience, and personal fulfillment. It can foster a healthier approach to personal development, promote higher levels of life satisfaction, and support a more consistent and rewarding gratitude practice.

The Grateful Heart: Strengthening Relationships Through Gratitude

"Let us be grateful to the people who make us happy; they are the charming gardeners who make our souls blossom." - Marcel Proust*

Gratitude in Romantic Relationships: Enhancing Intimacy and Connection

The Role of Gratitude in Romantic Relationships: Gratitude can play a pivotal role in romantic relationships by fostering feelings of connectedness and satisfaction. This sentiment can encourage partners to appreciate one another's efforts, thereby improving the quality of their interactions and deepening their bond.

Expressing Gratitude to a Partner: Expressing gratitude to a partner can be as simple as acknowledging their efforts and showing appreciation for their qualities. These expressions can be verbal or non-verbal and can significantly enhance the feelings of intimacy and understanding between partners.

The Impact of Gratitude on Relationship Satisfaction: Research suggests that gratitude can boost relationship satisfaction by promoting positive relationship behaviors, such as forgiveness and conflict resolution, and by fostering a positive cycle of generosity and appreciation.

Gratitude and Relationship Resilience: Gratitude can also contribute to relationship resilience by helping partners to focus on the positive aspects of their relationship, even in times of stress or disagreement. This can foster a stronger, more resilient bond that can weather the ups and downs of life.

Cultivating Gratitude in a Relationship: Cultivating gratitude in a relationship involves regular expressions of appreciation, creating shared experiences of thankfulness, and fostering a culture of gratitude within the relationship. This can involve simple daily practices, such as keeping a shared gratitude journal or expressing thanks for each other every day.

Cultivating Gratitude in Friendships: Deepening Bonds and Building Trust

Gratitude in Friendships: In friendships, gratitude can serve as a powerful tool for deepening bonds, building trust, and increasing feelings of closeness and satisfaction. Expressions of gratitude can create a positive feedback loop, reinforcing the friendship and fostering a deeper sense of connection.

Expressing Gratitude in Friendships: Expressing gratitude in friendships can be done in many ways, including verbal acknowledgements, written notes, or thoughtful gestures. These acts can help to show appreciation and reinforce the value of friendship.

Gratitude and Trust in Friendships: Gratitude can enhance trust in friendships by fostering a sense of reciprocity and goodwill. When gratitude is expressed, it can help to strengthen the bond between friends and foster a more trusting, stable relationship.

The Impact of Gratitude on Friendship Satisfaction: Similar to romantic relationships, gratitude can also positively impact friendship satisfaction. By fostering an attitude of appreciation, gratitude can help friends to see the positive aspects of their relationship, thereby increasing their overall satisfaction.

Building a Gratitude Practice in Friendships: Building a gratitude practice in friendships can involve regular expressions of thanks, sharing positive experiences, and fostering a culture of gratitude. This can create a stronger, more resilient friendship that is able to navigate the challenges of life.

Gratitude in Family Relationships: Fostering Harmony and Reducing Conflict

The Role of Gratitude in Family Relationships: In family relationships, gratitude can act as a buffer against conflict and negativity. By focusing on the positive aspects of the family and expressing gratitude for one another, family members can create a more harmonious and supportive environment.

Expressing Gratitude in a Family Setting: Gratitude in a family setting can be expressed in many ways, from simple verbal acknowledgements to acts of kindness. These actions can help to foster a sense of appreciation and respect among family members.

Gratitude and Family Harmony: Research has shown that families that practice gratitude regularly experience less conflict and more harmony. This is likely due to the positive effect gratitude has on our emotions and behaviors, encouraging more positive interactions within the family.

The Impact of Gratitude on Family Satisfaction: Gratitude can boost family satisfaction by encouraging family members to appreciate each other's efforts and to focus on the positive aspects of their family life. This can lead to a greater sense of satisfaction and well-being among family members.

Cultivating a Culture of Gratitude in the Family: Cultivating a culture of gratitude in the family involves regular expressions of appreciation, sharing of positive experiences, and fostering an environment of gratitude. This could include keeping a family gratitude journal, verbally expressing thanks at mealtimes, or creating gratitude-focused rituals and traditions.

Gratitude in the Workplace: Boosting Morale and Productivity

The Role of Gratitude in the Workplace: Gratitude in the workplace can foster a positive work environment, improve employee satisfaction, and boost productivity. When employees feel appreciated, they are more likely to be engaged, motivated, and committed to their work.

Expressing Gratitude at Work: Expressing gratitude at work can take many forms, from a simple thank-you email to a formal recognition program. Regardless of how it's expressed, gratitude can have a profound impact on workplace dynamics and employee morale.

The Impact of Gratitude on Employee Satisfaction and Performance: Studies have shown that expressions of gratitude can boost employee satisfaction and performance. When employees feel valued and appreciated, they are more likely to put forth their best effort and to be more productive.

Gratitude and Workplace Culture: A culture of gratitude in the workplace can foster a more positive and supportive work environment. This can lead to lower turnover rates, higher job satisfaction, and increased productivity.

Cultivating a Culture of Gratitude in the Workplace: Cultivating a culture of gratitude in the workplace involves creating opportunities for employees to express and receive gratitude. This could involve implementing a peer recognition program, promoting regular expressions of thanks, or training leaders to express gratitude effectively.

Gratitude in Communities: Building Stronger and More Connected Communities

The Role of Gratitude in Communities: Gratitude can play a significant role in building stronger and more connected communities. By fostering a sense of appreciation and mutual respect, gratitude can help to strengthen social bonds and foster a sense of community.

Expressing Gratitude in a Community Setting: Expressing gratitude in a community setting can take many forms, from acknowledging the efforts of community volunteers to organizing community appreciation events. These expressions of gratitude can help to foster a sense of community pride and cohesion.

The Impact of Gratitude on Community Well-being: Studies suggest that communities that foster a culture of gratitude tend to have higher levels of well-being. Gratitude can help to foster positive community relations, reduce conflict, and promote a sense of belonging.

Gratitude and Community Resilience: Gratitude can also contribute to community resilience by helping individuals and communities to focus on the positive aspects of their community, even in the face of adversity. This focus on the positive can help to foster a sense of hope and resilience.

Cultivating a Culture of Gratitude in a Community: Cultivating a culture of gratitude in a community involves promoting expressions of gratitude, creating opportunities for community members to give back, and fostering a sense of appreciation for the community and its members. This can help to create a stronger, more resilient, and more connected community.

Gratitude and Resilience: Navigating Life's Challenges with Grace and Appreciation

esilience isn't just about surviving challenges, but thriving because of them. And gratitude plays a crucial role.

The Role of Gratitude in Overcoming Adversity

How gratitude helps in dealing with life's challenges: Gratitude is a powerful tool in dealing with life's challenges. It redirects our focus from what's wrong to what's right, helping us to maintain a positive perspective even in difficult times. It's a way of acknowledging the good in our lives, which can provide a sense of comfort and hope when things seem tough[1].

Gratitude: A resilience booster: Resilience is the ability to recover from setbacks, adapt well to change, and keep going in the face of adversity. Gratitude enhances resilience by helping us to see the positives in a situation, even when they're not immediately apparent. It allows us to appreciate the lessons learned from adversity and grow from them[2].

Using gratitude to transform adversity into an opportunity for growth: Gratitude allows us to see adversity as an opportunity for growth. By appreciating what we have, we can find strength in the midst of struggle and use it as a steppingstone towards personal development and self-improvement.

The role of gratitude in stress management and coping: Gratitude can help us manage stress by shifting our focus from negative thoughts to positive ones. This can lead to a more optimistic outlook, reduced stress levels, and better coping strategies.

Building resilience through a gratitude practice: Regular practice of gratitude, such as keeping a gratitude journal or expressing thanks to others, can build resilience over time. This practice helps us to maintain a positive perspective and bounce back from adversity more quickly.

Gratitude as a Coping Mechanism

Gratitude and its role in coping with stress and adversity: Gratitude can act as a buffer against stress and adversity. By focusing on what we're grateful for, we can reduce negative emotions, increase positive emotions, and improve our overall psychological well-being.

How gratitude can improve emotional resilience: Gratitude can enhance emotional resilience by promoting a positive outlook and a sense of contentment, even in the face of adversity. By acknowledging the good in our lives, we can better handle emotional distress and bounce back from negative experiences.

Cultivating gratitude as a positive coping strategy: Gratitude can be cultivated as a positive coping strategy through various practices, such as maintaining a gratitude journal, expressing thanks to others, and mindfully reflecting on the positives in our lives. These practices can help us deal with stress and adversity more effectively.

The therapeutic power of gratitude in challenging times: Gratitude can have therapeutic effects, especially in challenging times. It can promote psychological well-being, enhance self-esteem, and reduce depressive symptoms. It can also improve our relationships and enhance our overall quality of life.

Gratitude: A tool for managing mental health difficulties: Gratitude can be a valuable tool for managing mental health difficulties. Research has shown that gratitude interventions can have positive effects on mental health, including reducing symptoms of depression and anxiety.

Gratitude in Building and Maintaining Relationships

Gratitude as a bridge in relationships: Gratitude can act as a bridge in relationships, fostering a deeper connection between individuals. When we express gratitude to others, we acknowledge their value and affirm their positive impact on our lives.

The role of gratitude in relationship satisfaction: Gratitude can significantly influence relationship satisfaction. By focusing on the positive aspects of the relationship and expressing gratitude for them, couples can increase their satisfaction and happiness in the relationship.

Gratitude and its impact on social bonds: Gratitude can strengthen social bonds. By expressing gratitude, we can enhance our relationships and foster a sense of belonging and community. Gratitude can also promote prosocial behavior, further strengthening social bonds.

Using gratitude to repair and improve relationships: Gratitude can be used to repair and improve relationships. By expressing gratitude, we can address issues and misunderstandings, reinforce positive aspects, and foster a sense of mutual appreciation in the relationship.

Building stronger relationships through a gratitude practice: Practicing gratitude regularly can help build stronger relationships. This can be done through verbal expressions of thanks, written gratitude letters, or simply reflecting on the positive aspects of the relationship·

The Transformative Power of Gratitude

Gratitude and personal growth: Gratitude can contribute to personal growth by helping us appreciate the value of our experiences, both good and bad. This appreciation can open up opportunities for learning, understanding, and growth.

How gratitude can lead to positive change: Gratitude can lead to positive change by shifting our focus from what's wrong to what's right, and from what we lack to what we have. This shift in focus can create a more positive mindset, which can motivate us to take positive actions and bring about positive change.

The role of gratitude in self-improvement: Gratitude can play a significant role in self-improvement. By appreciating what we have, we can foster a sense of contentment and satisfaction, which can motivate us to strive for better.

Gratitude and its influence on perspective: Gratitude can influence our perspective by helping us see the good in our lives. This can lead to a more positive outlook, a greater appreciation for life, and an enhanced sense of well-being.

Transforming life through the practice of gratitude: Regular practice of gratitude can transform our lives by promoting happiness, enhancing relationships, boosting resilience, and fostering personal growth. This transformation can lead to a more fulfilling and meaningful life.

Gratitude as a Resilience Booster

Understanding resilience: Resilience is the capacity to recover quickly from difficulties; it's a sort of emotional elasticity. It's about being able to bounce back from stressful or traumatic experiences and maintain a positive outlook. Resilience doesn't eliminate life's difficulties, but it provides individuals with the strength to tackle problems head-on and overcome adversity.

The connection between gratitude and resilience: There is a growing body of evidence that suggests a strong connection between gratitude and resilience. Gratitude can act as a buffer against stress by helping individuals focus on the positive aspects of their lives. This positive focus can help to lessen the impact of negative events and increase the ability to cope with adversity[2].

Gratitude as a coping mechanism: Gratitude can be used as a coping mechanism during difficult times. By focusing on the things we are grateful for, we can shift our focus away from our problems and towards the positive aspects of our lives. This can help to alleviate feelings of stress and anxiety and improve our overall well-being[3].

The role of gratitude in post-traumatic growth: Post-traumatic growth is the experience of positive change that occurs as a result of the struggle with highly challenging life crises. Gratitude has been found to play a significant role in post-traumatic growth by helping individuals find meaning in their experiences and fostering a sense of personal strength[4].

Practicing gratitude to build resilience: Regular practice of gratitude can help to build resilience by encouraging a positive outlook and enhancing the ability to cope with stress. This can be done through various gratitude exercises, such as keeping a gratitude journal, writing gratitude letters, or simply taking time each day to reflect on the things you are grateful for.

Gratitude and its Effect on Interpersonal Relationships

Understanding interpersonal relationships: Interpersonal relationships are social connections, associations, or affiliations between two or more people. They can vary in levels of intimacy and sharing, implying the discovery or establishment of common ground, and may be centered around something shared in common.

Gratitude and relationship satisfaction: Gratitude in the context of interpersonal relationships often leads to higher relationship satisfaction. This is because expressing gratitude can enhance our relationships with others, making us feel more connected and satisfied. It can also make others feel appreciated and valued, which can strengthen the bond and improve the overall quality of the relationship.

Gratitude as a social glue: Gratitude can serve as a 'social glue' that helps to build and maintain social relationships. When we express gratitude to others, it can make them feel appreciated and recognized, which can foster stronger connections. Moreover, gratitude can inspire us to reciprocate the kindness we have received, promoting a cycle of positive interactions.

The role of gratitude in conflict resolution: Gratitude can also play a role in conflict resolution. When individuals approach conflicts with an attitude of gratitude, they may be more likely to seek compromise and understanding. This can help to reduce the severity of conflicts and improve the overall health of the relationship.

Practicing gratitude in relationships: Practicing gratitude in relationships can take many forms, from simply saying "thank you" more often, to more intentional practices like keeping a gratitude journal focused on the positive aspects of your relationships. Other practices could include writing a letter of gratitude to a loved one, or making it a point to express gratitude for your partner daily.

The Mind-Body Connection: How Gratitude Impacts Physical and Emotional Well-being

S tudies have shown that gratitude exercises can reduce depression, lower blood pressure, and improve immune function.

Gratitude and Mental Health

The link between gratitude and mental health: Gratitude has been increasingly recognized for its beneficial effects on mental health. It involves recognizing and appreciating the positive aspects of life, which can shift our focus from negative emotions to more positive ones. This can lead to an overall improvement in mood and well-being. Several studies have found that gratitude can reduce symptoms of depression and anxiety, increase happiness, and even enhance life satisfaction (Wood et al., 2010).

How practicing gratitude can help manage anxiety and depression: When we practice gratitude regularly, it can help us manage anxiety and depression. This is because gratitude can shift our focus from what's wrong in our lives to what's going well. It also encourages a more positive outlook, which is beneficial in managing mental health conditions like anxiety and depression. Regular gratitude practice has been shown to result in lower levels of stress and depression, higher levels of social support, and greater satisfaction with life (Wood, Froh, & Geraghty, 2010).

Gratitude: A tool for emotional regulation and mental stability: Gratitude plays a critical role in emotional regulation. By focusing on what we are grateful for, we can manage our negative emotions more effectively and maintain emotional balance. Gratitude can also help us cope with stress and adversity, leading to greater mental stability. A study by Emmons and McCullough (2003) showed that practicing gratitude can increase happiness and reduce depressive symptoms, demonstrating its role in emotional regulation.

The role of gratitude in promoting positive thinking and optimism: Gratitude can foster a more optimistic outlook on life by helping us focus on the positive aspects of our experiences, even in the face of adversity. This optimistic mindset is associated with better physical and mental health and can enhance our resilience in difficult times. Research has shown that gratitude is strongly related to life satisfaction and optimism (Alkozei, Smith, Killgore, 2018).

Cultivating mental wellness through a gratitude practice: Cultivating a gratitude practice involves intentionally expressing thanks and appreciation in your daily life. This could be through keeping a gratitude journal, verbalizing your appreciation to others, or simply taking time each day to reflect on what you're grateful for. Such a practice can lead to increased positivity, improved mood, and better overall mental health. As gratitude is practiced and cultivated, individuals may experience decreased levels of depression and anxiety, and improved sleep quality (Jackowska, Brown, Ronaldson, & Steptoe, 2016).

Physical Health Benefits

The impact of gratitude on physical health: Gratitude is not only beneficial for mental health, but it also has significant implications for physical health. Research suggests that people who regularly practice gratitude are more likely to engage in healthy behaviors, such as regular exercise and routine medical check-ups. Furthermore, they tend to experience fewer physical symptoms, such as pain, and report feeling healthier than their less grateful counterparts. Gratitude can also reduce levels of stress and depression, which are often linked to poor physical health (Emmons & McCullough, 2003).

How gratitude can enhance sleep quality, immune function, and pain management: Gratitude can contribute to better sleep by promoting positive bedtime cognitions. It has been found that those who practice gratitude have longer sleep duration, spend less time awake before falling asleep, and feel more refreshed upon waking. Moreover, gratitude practices have been linked with improved immune function, possibly as a result of reduced stress and improved mental state. It can also play a role in pain management, with grateful people reporting less pain and being more likely to take active steps to address it (Jackowska, Brown, Ronaldson, & Steptoe, 2016).

Gratitude and its role in promoting healthy lifestyle habits: Gratitude can be a motivating factor for individuals to maintain healthy lifestyle habits. Grateful people are more likely to take care of their health, eat a balanced diet, exercise regularly, and schedule regular check-ups with their doctors. This may be because gratitude enhances an individual's appreciation for their body, motivating them to take better care of it (Emmons & McCullough, 2003).

The therapeutic power of gratitude in physical healing: Gratitude can play a therapeutic role in physical healing. It can help individuals better cope with illness and recovery, reduce symptoms and improve health outcomes. By shifting focus from illness to appreciation, gratitude can serve as a psychological resource for coping with disease and treatment side effects (Dunn, Whelton, & Pouwer, 2017).

Incorporating gratitude into your health and wellness routine: Incorporating gratitude into a health and wellness routine can be as simple as keeping a daily gratitude journal, expressing thanks to others, or meditating on what you're thankful for. Regularly practicing these activities can boost your mood, increase feelings of well-being, improve your sleep, and enhance your overall physical health.

Gratitude and Nutrition

The role of gratitude in mindful eating and nutrition: Practicing gratitude can promote mindful eating, which refers to being fully attentive to your experiences, cravings, and physical cues when eating. Gratitude can help individuals appreciate the food they consume, acknowledging the effort, time, and resources that go into its preparation. This awareness can reduce overeating and impulsive food choices, promoting healthier eating habits.

How gratitude can enhance the enjoyment and appreciation of food: Gratitude can enhance the enjoyment of food by encouraging us to savor each bite and appreciate the flavors, textures, and aromas. This heightened appreciation can lead to a greater sense of satisfaction and fullness, reducing the tendency to overeat.

Gratitude: A tool for promoting healthy eating habits: By encouraging mindfulness, gratitude can lead to healthier eating habits. It can help individuals make more conscious food choices, prefer quality over quantity, and appreciate the nutrients that food provides to the body. In this way, gratitude can serve as a tool for maintaining a balanced diet and preventing overindulgence.

The impact of gratitude on our relationship with food: Gratitude can help transform one's relationship with food from one of guilt or obligation to one of appreciation and enjoyment. It can help individuals see food not merely as a source of calories but as a gift that nourishes and sustains life.

Cultivating a healthy approach to nutrition through gratitude: One can cultivate a healthy approach to nutrition through gratitude by regularly expressing thanks for their food, acknowledging its source, appreciating its flavors, and recognizing its role in sustaining health. This practice can foster a healthier relationship with food and encourage more nutritious eating habits.

Gratitude and Exercise

The link between gratitude and motivation for physical activity: Gratitude can boost motivation for physical activity. Recognizing the benefits of exercise and being thankful for the ability to move can inspire individuals to engage in regular physical activity. Gratitude can also help individuals appreciate the progress they make in their fitness journey, further fueling their motivation.

How gratitude can enhance the enjoyment of exercise: Gratitude can make exercise more enjoyable by shifting the focus from the discomfort of exercise to the benefits it provides, such as increased energy, improved mood, and better health. This can help individuals maintain a consistent exercise routine.

Gratitude: A tool for fostering a positive attitude towards physical fitness: By focusing on the positive aspects of exercise, gratitude can foster a more positive attitude towards physical fitness. It can help individuals overcome obstacles, persist in the face of challenges, and view exercise as a rewarding and enjoyable activity rather than a chore.

The role of gratitude in maintaining exercise consistency: Gratitude can play a crucial role in maintaining exercise consistency. By fostering a positive attitude towards exercise and enhancing enjoyment, gratitude can encourage individuals to stick with their fitness routines, even when faced with obstacles.

Incorporating gratitude into your fitness routine: Incorporating gratitude into a fitness routine can be as simple as taking a moment to appreciate the ability to move before, during, or after a workout. It can also involve expressing thanks for the progress made, the effort exerted, and the benefits gained from exercise. These practices can enhance enjoyment, boost motivation, and foster a positive attitude towards physical fitness.

The Interconnectedness of Gratitude

The holistic benefits of gratitude: Mind, body, and spirit: Gratitude can have a profound impact on one's overall health, encompassing the mind, body, and spirit. On a mental level, it can boost mood, reduce stress, and foster positivity. Physically, it can encourage healthier habits and improve bodily functions like sleep and immune response. Spiritually, gratitude can deepen one's sense of connectedness, purpose, and fulfillment in life.

How gratitude can promote overall well-being and balance: Gratitude can promote balance by encouraging individuals to focus on the positive aspects of their lives, rather than dwelling on negatives or stressors. It fosters an appreciation for what one has, which can create a more balanced perspective on life's ups and downs. This balanced perspective can enhance overall well-being by reducing stress, improving mental health, and promoting satisfaction with life.

Gratitude: A tool for holistic health and wellness: As a tool for holistic health, gratitude can have far-reaching effects. It can inspire healthier behaviors, like regular exercise and mindful eating, and improve mental health through increased positivity and reduced stress. Furthermore, by fostering a sense of connectedness and appreciation for life, gratitude can enhance spiritual wellness.

The role of gratitude in maintaining harmony and balance: Gratitude plays a crucial role in maintaining harmony and balance by fostering a positive outlook and appreciation for life's blessings. This attitude can help individuals navigate life's challenges with greater ease and resilience, promoting a sense of balance and harmony in the face of adversity.

Cultivating a holistic gratitude practice: Cultivating a holistic gratitude practice involves incorporating gratitude into various aspects of daily life. This might include expressing thanks for meals, appreciating the body during exercise, writing in a gratitude journal, or simply taking a moment each day to reflect on the positive aspects of life. Over time, these practices can encourage a more balanced perspective, promote overall well-being, and foster a deep sense of fulfillment.

Gratitude at Work: Creating a Positive and Supportive Professional Environment

I*t is said that employees who feel appreciated by their superiors are 50% more motivated to perform their tasks effectively.*

The Impact of Gratitude on Workplace Culture

The role of gratitude in shaping a positive workplace culture: Gratitude can shape a positive workplace culture by fostering an atmosphere of appreciation and mutual respect. When employees feel valued and appreciated, they are more likely to engage in positive behaviors and show greater commitment to their work.

How expressing gratitude can improve employee morale and satisfaction: Expressing gratitude can boost morale and satisfaction by making employees feel valued and recognized for their contributions. This can increase job satisfaction, reduce turnover, and improve overall workplace morale.

Gratitude: A tool for fostering teamwork and collaboration: Gratitude can foster teamwork by creating a sense of shared purpose and mutual respect among team members. When team members express gratitude to each other, it can strengthen relationships and promote collaboration.

The impact of gratitude on workplace relationships and interactions: Gratitude can have a positive impact on workplace relationships by fostering a culture of appreciation and respect. This can lead to improved interactions, increased cooperation, and a more positive and productive work environment.

Cultivating a culture of gratitude in the workplace: Cultivating a culture of gratitude in the workplace involves encouraging employees to regularly express appreciation for their colleagues and their work. This could include implementing gratitude-based activities or practices, such as gratitude journals, thank-you notes, or regular team-building exercises that promote gratitude.

Building a Gratitude Practice Among Coworkers

The benefits of a shared gratitude practice in the workplace: A shared gratitude practice in the workplace can lead to increased cooperation, improved morale, and a more positive and productive work environment. It can also strengthen relationships among coworkers and foster a sense of community and belonging.

How gratitude can foster a supportive and cooperative work environment: By fostering a sense of appreciation and mutual respect, gratitude can create a supportive and cooperative work environment. It encourages employees to help and support each other, leading to increased cooperation and teamwork.

Gratitude: A tool for enhancing communication and understanding among coworkers: Gratitude can enhance communication by promoting a positive and respectful dialogue. When employees express gratitude to each other, it can help to foster understanding and empathy, leading to improved communication and fewer misunderstandings.

The role of gratitude in conflict resolution at work: Gratitude can play a role in conflict resolution by fostering a sense of appreciation and understanding. By focusing on the positive aspects of a situation or person, it can help to diffuse tension and promote a more constructive and cooperative approach to resolving conflicts.

Implementing a gratitude practice in your team or organization: Implementing a gratitude practice can involve a variety of strategies, such as encouraging employees to express gratitude to each other regularly, implementing gratitude-based activities, or providing training and resources on the benefits and practices of gratitude. This can foster a culture of appreciation and positivity, leading to a more positive and productive work environment.

Gratitude in Leadership

The importance of gratitude in effective leadership: Gratitude plays a pivotal role in effective leadership. Leaders who express gratitude towards their team members tend to foster a more positive and engaged work environment. This act of appreciation can motivate employees, improve team morale, and, consequently, enhance overall productivity.

How expressing gratitude can enhance a leader's influence and effectiveness: When leaders express gratitude, they often earn the respect and trust of their team members. This act can strengthen relationships, improve communication, and increase cooperation within the team. As a result, leaders become more influential and effective in their roles.

Gratitude: A tool for fostering trust and respect in leadership: Gratitude can be a powerful tool for building trust and respect. By acknowledging the efforts and contributions of team members, leaders show that they value and respect their work. This recognition can foster a culture of trust, where employees feel secure and confident in their roles.

The role of gratitude in leadership development: Gratitude can play a critical role in leadership development. It encourages leaders to focus on the positive aspects of their team members' performance, which can help to foster a more supportive and constructive leadership style. Moreover, gratitude can enhance emotional intelligence, a key component of effective leadership.

Cultivating gratitude as a leader: Cultivating gratitude as a leader involves consciously acknowledging and appreciating the efforts and achievements of team members. This could be done through verbal recognition, written notes of thanks, or even through formal recognition programs. It's about creating a culture where appreciation and positivity are the norms.

Boosting Employee Engagement and Satisfaction Through Gratitude

The role of gratitude in enhancing employee engagement and satisfaction: Gratitude can significantly enhance employee engagement and satisfaction. When employees feel valued and appreciated for their work, they tend to be more committed, motivated, and satisfied in their roles.

How expressing gratitude can improve job satisfaction and performance: Expressing gratitude can have a positive impact on job satisfaction and performance. When employees receive recognition for their efforts, they often feel a greater sense of accomplishment, which can boost morale and motivate them to maintain or improve their performance.

Gratitude: A tool for employee retention and loyalty: Gratitude can help to increase employee retention and loyalty. Employees who feel appreciated are more likely to stay with the organization and show greater commitment to their roles. This loyalty can lead to lower turnover rates and a more stable, engaged workforce.

The impact of gratitude on employee motivation and productivity: Gratitude can boost employee motivation and productivity. Recognizing and appreciating employees' efforts can inspire them to put forth their best work, leading to increased productivity. Furthermore, a positive and appreciative work environment can enhance overall work morale, further boosting motivation.

Cultivating an atmosphere of appreciation in the workplace: Cultivating an atmosphere of appreciation involves consistently expressing gratitude and recognition for employees' efforts and achievements. This could be done through a variety of channels such as verbal praise, written notes, recognition in team meetings, or through formal recognition programs. By regularly acknowledging and appreciating employees, organizations can foster a positive and engaging work environment.

Navigating Workplace Challenges with a Grateful Mindset

The role of gratitude in managing workplace stress and challenges: Gratitude can be a powerful tool in managing workplace stress and challenges. By focusing on the positive aspects of work and acknowledging the good, employees can shift their perspective and mitigate the impacts of stress and adversity. Regular practice of gratitude can also foster a more positive and supportive work environment, which can in turn help in managing workplace challenges.

How gratitude can foster resilience and adaptability at work: Gratitude helps in fostering resilience by allowing individuals to appreciate what they have, even in difficult situations. This shift in focus from negative to positive can help build emotional resilience, enabling individuals to better adapt to changes or challenges at work. Regular practice of gratitude can make employees more resilient and adaptable in the face of workplace adversity.

Gratitude: A tool for problem-solving and decision-making: By fostering a positive mindset, gratitude can also enhance problem-solving and decision-making skills. When individuals are in a positive state of mind, they are more likely to approach problems with a solution-oriented mindset, think creatively, and make better decisions. Furthermore, gratitude can encourage open communication and collaboration, which are key to effective problem-solving and decision-making in the workplace.

The impact of gratitude on workplace wellbeing and mental health: Gratitude has a significant impact on workplace wellbeing and mental health. By acknowledging the good things at work and expressing appreciation for them, employees can improve their mood, reduce stress levels, and increase their job satisfaction. Over time, these benefits can lead to improved mental health, reducing the risk of burnout and other work-related mental health issues.

Cultivating resilience at work through a gratitude practice: Cultivating a gratitude practice at work can help employees build resilience. By regularly acknowledging and expressing appreciation for the positive aspects of their work, employees can shift their focus away from the challenges and stressors, fostering a more positive and resilient mindset. This practice can be as simple as keeping a gratitude journal, starting team meetings with a round of appreciations, or sending a regular thank-you note to a colleague.

Parenting with Gratitude: Fostering Appreciation and Empathy in Children

"*If the only prayer you said was 'thank you,' that would be enough.*"
- Meister Eckart

The Importance of Gratitude in Childhood Development

The role of gratitude in a child's emotional and social development: Gratitude plays a significant role in a child's emotional and social development. It aids children in recognizing and appreciating the positive aspects of their lives, thereby fostering positive emotions. Socially, children who practice gratitude tend to be more generous, helpful, and empathetic, building stronger relationships with peers.

How gratitude can foster a positive self-concept in children: By practicing gratitude, children can develop a positive self-concept. Acknowledging the good in their lives can help them feel more content and satisfied, boosting their self-esteem. Additionally, the process of expressing gratitude to others can reinforce their self-worth and the value they bring to relationships.

Gratitude: A tool for teaching values and empathy to children: Gratitude can be a powerful tool for teaching important values like kindness, generosity, and empathy. When children are encouraged to express gratitude, they are also learning to consider the feelings and efforts of others, building their capacity for empathy.

The impact of gratitude on a child's mental health and well-being: Research suggests that gratitude can have a positive impact on a child's mental health and overall well-being. Children who regularly practice gratitude tend to have lower levels of stress and depression and exhibit higher levels of happiness and satisfaction.

Cultivating gratitude in children from an early age: Cultivating gratitude from an early age can have long-term benefits for children. This can start with simple practices like encouraging children to say, "thank you," helping them recognize the good in their lives, and modelling gratitude in daily life.

Teaching Gratitude to Children

Effective methods for teaching gratitude to children: There are several effective methods for teaching gratitude to children. This could include regular discussions about what they're thankful for, incorporating gratitude into bedtime routines, creating gratitude jars or boards, and encouraging thank-you notes.

How gratitude can be incorporated into everyday parenting practices: Parents can incorporate gratitude into daily routines by expressing their own gratitude regularly, discussing the good things that happened each day, and acknowledging when the child demonstrates gratitude.

Gratitude: A tool for teaching children to appreciate the good in their lives: By encouraging gratitude, parents can help children focus on the positive aspects of their lives, fostering a sense of contentment and happiness.

The role of modeling gratitude in fostering appreciation in children: Children learn by observing the behaviors of those around them. When parents model gratitude—expressing thankfulness for what they have and acknowledging the efforts of others—children are more likely to adopt these behaviors.

Developing age-appropriate gratitude practices for children: It's important to adapt gratitude practices to be age-appropriate. For younger children, this might involve saying "thank you" and drawing pictures of things they're thankful for. As children get older, practices can evolve to include writing gratitude letters, keeping a gratitude journal, and engaging in acts of kindness.

Gratitude and Empathy

The link between gratitude and empathy in children: Gratitude and empathy are interconnected. When children express gratitude, they're recognizing and appreciating the kindness of others, which inherently involves understanding and sharing the feelings of others – the definition of empathy. Gratitude can thus be seen as an avenue for children to develop their empathic skills.

How gratitude can foster emotional intelligence in children: Emotional intelligence involves recognizing, understanding, and managing one's own emotions and the emotions of others. When children practice gratitude, they're not only identifying positive emotions in themselves but also acknowledging the actions of others that led to those positive feelings. This process can help children develop a deeper understanding of emotions and how they work.

Gratitude: A tool for teaching children to value others: Gratitude can serve as a powerful tool for teaching children to value and appreciate others. When children express gratitude, they're acknowledging the value that others bring to their lives, which can foster a greater appreciation for others and promote healthier interpersonal relationships.

The role of gratitude in fostering kindness and generosity in children: By practicing gratitude, children can become more aware of the kindness and generosity of others, which can inspire them to act similarly. In this way, gratitude can foster the development of kindness and generosity in children.

Cultivating empathy in children through gratitude practices: Parents and educators can cultivate empathy in children through gratitude practices. This can involve encouraging children to think about the feelings and efforts of those they are thankful for, promoting an empathic perspective.

Modeling Gratitude as a Parent

The importance of modeling gratitude as a parent: Children often learn by observing and mimicking the behaviors of their parents. When parents model gratitude—through expressing appreciation for others, acknowledging the good in their lives, and demonstrating a positive attitude—they're showing their children how to practice gratitude in their own lives.

How demonstrating gratitude can influence a child's attitudes and behaviors: When parents regularly demonstrate gratitude, it can influence their child's attitudes and behaviors. Children may learn to focus more on the positive aspects of their lives, show more appreciation for others, and exhibit more generous and helpful behaviors.

Gratitude: A tool for promoting positive parent-child relationships: Gratitude can be a powerful tool for promoting positive parent-child relationships. When parents express gratitude to and in front of their children, it can foster a positive family atmosphere, promote open communication, and model respectful behavior.

The role of parental gratitude in setting a positive example for children: Parental gratitude can set a positive example for children. When parents express gratitude, they're showing their children that it's important to appreciate the good in life and to acknowledge the kindness and efforts of others. This example can encourage children to adopt similar attitudes and behaviors.

Cultivating your own gratitude practice as a parent: Cultivating your own gratitude practice as a parent not only benefits your own well-being, but can also serve as a model for your children. This practice could involve keeping a gratitude journal, expressing appreciation for others regularly, and making a point to acknowledge the good in each day.

Navigating Parenting Challenges with Gratitude and Compassion

The role of gratitude in managing parenting stress and challenges: Parenting can be stressful and filled with numerous challenges. However, maintaining a sense of gratitude can help manage this stress. By focusing on the positive aspects of parenting and the joy children bring, parents can better cope with difficulties and maintain a balanced perspective.

How gratitude can foster a positive parenting mindset: Gratitude can help foster a more positive mindset in parenting. By acknowledging and appreciating the good moments, parents can cultivate a more optimistic outlook, which can affect how they respond to challenging situations. It can shift the focus from what's going wrong to what's going right, enhancing overall parental satisfaction.

Gratitude: A tool for maintaining patience and understanding as a parent: Parenting often requires a great deal of patience and understanding. Gratitude can be a useful tool in maintaining these qualities. When parents express gratitude for their children and the unique moments they experience, it can foster a sense of patience and understanding, even in the face of challenging behaviors or situations.

The impact of gratitude on parental well-being and satisfaction: Studies have shown that maintaining a sense of gratitude can have a significant impact on well-being and satisfaction. For parents, expressing gratitude for their children and the joys of parenting can increase happiness, reduce stress, and promote a more satisfying parenting experience.

Cultivating resilience in parenting through a gratitude practice: Resilience, the ability to cope with and bounce back from adversity, is a critical skill in parenting. A gratitude practice can help cultivate this resilience. By regularly focusing on the positive and expressing gratitude, parents can build a stronger emotional foundation, enabling them to navigate the ups and downs of parenting with greater ease.

The Art of Grateful Communication: Expressing Appreciation in Words and Actions

A simple 'thank you' can change someone's day, strengthen a relationship, or even bridge a divide.

The Power of Thank You

The significance of expressing gratitude verbally: Verbal expressions of gratitude, such as saying "Thank You," are essential because they directly communicate appreciation and acknowledgment to others. They validate the kindness, effort, or thoughtfulness of others and express a sense of value and respect.

How a simple 'Thank You' can impact relationships and well-being: A simple 'Thank You' can have a profound impact on relationships and well-being. It fosters positive feelings, strengthens relationships, and enhances a sense of belonging and connectedness. Moreover, it can increase personal happiness and satisfaction, as expressing gratitude triggers positive emotions.

Gratitude: A tool for fostering open and positive communication: Expressing gratitude is a powerful tool for fostering open and positive communication. It encourages a more positive environment, promotes more meaningful conversations, and builds trust. Furthermore, it can lead to improved understanding and collaboration, which are key for successful relationships.

The role of verbal gratitude in maintaining good relationships: Verbal gratitude plays a significant role in maintaining good relationships. It validates the efforts of others, fosters mutual respect, and strengthens bonds. Regularly expressing gratitude can also reduce conflict and enhance the overall quality of relationships.

Cultivating the habit of expressing gratitude regularly: Cultivating the habit of expressing gratitude regularly can have lasting positive effects. It can improve personal happiness, enhance relationships, and promote a more positive and fulfilling life. Simple practices like keeping a gratitude journal or making it a point to express appreciation daily can help cultivate this habit.

Non-verbal Gratitude

The importance of showing gratitude through actions: Non-verbal expressions of gratitude are just as important as verbal ones. Actions can often speak louder than words, and demonstrating gratitude through actions can effectively convey appreciation in a tangible way.

How non-verbal expressions of gratitude can enrich relationships: Non-verbal expressions of gratitude can significantly enrich relationships. Actions such as giving a thoughtful gift, spending quality time, or doing something kind for someone can communicate appreciation in a profound way. These actions can enhance the depth and quality of relationships.

Gratitude: A tool for showing appreciation beyond words: Gratitude can be a powerful tool for showing appreciation beyond words. Non-verbal expressions of gratitude, such as thoughtful gestures, acts of kindness, or gifts, can communicate gratitude effectively and can sometimes convey more than what words can express.

The role of actions in expressing genuine gratitude: Actions play a crucial role in expressing genuine gratitude. They provide a concrete demonstration of appreciation and can often communicate it more effectively than words alone. By aligning words of gratitude with actions, the sincerity of the sentiment is strengthened.

Cultivating the habit of showing gratitude in your actions: Cultivating the habit of showing gratitude through actions is beneficial. It not only expresses appreciation effectively but also fosters positive behaviors and strengthens relationships. Regularly practicing acts of kindness, being thoughtful towards others, and going out of your way to express appreciation can all contribute to this habit.

Gratitude in Conflict Resolution

The role of gratitude in resolving conflicts effectively: Gratitude plays a critical role in conflict resolution. It helps to shift focus from negative emotions and instead emphasizes positive aspects of the relationship. This change in perspective can lead to a more constructive and solution-oriented approach to conflict.

How expressing gratitude can facilitate understanding and reconciliation: Expressing gratitude during conflicts can facilitate understanding and reconciliation. Acknowledging the other person's perspective or efforts, even amidst disagreements, promotes a sense of respect and appreciation. This can reduce defensiveness and facilitate a more open and empathetic dialogue, aiding in reconciliation.

Gratitude: A tool for maintaining harmony in relationships: Gratitude is a powerful tool for maintaining harmony in relationships. Regular expressions of gratitude can foster a more positive environment, reducing the likelihood of conflicts. Even during disagreements, gratitude can help maintain a sense of goodwill and respect, promoting harmony.

The impact of gratitude on conflict management strategies: Gratitude can significantly impact conflict management strategies. It can encourage a more positive and understanding approach, reducing aggressiveness and promoting empathy. This can lead to more effective and satisfactory conflict resolutions.

Cultivating the practice of gratitude in conflict resolution: Cultivating the practice of gratitude in conflict resolution involves consciously incorporating gratitude into one's approach to disagreements. This might involve acknowledging the other person's efforts, focusing on the positive aspects of the relationship, or expressing appreciation for the opportunity to grow and learn from the conflict.

Gratitude in Writing

The power of expressing gratitude in written form: Expressing gratitude in written form is a powerful practice. It provides a tangible record of appreciation, which can be revisited and reflected upon. It also allows for a deeper and more thoughtful expression of gratitude, as writing provides the opportunity to articulate feelings in a considered and deliberate way.

How writing letters of gratitude can enhance well-being and relationships: Writing letters of gratitude can significantly enhance well-being and relationships. The act of writing such letters generates positive emotions, enhancing personal happiness and satisfaction. Additionally, receiving a written expression of gratitude can strengthen relationships, fostering a deeper sense of connection and appreciation.

Gratitude: A tool for maintaining connections and expressing deep appreciation: Gratitude, especially when expressed in writing, is a valuable tool for maintaining connections and expressing deep appreciation. A written note or letter of gratitude can convey a depth of appreciation that goes beyond everyday verbal expressions, fostering stronger and more meaningful connections.

The role of written gratitude in personal reflection and growth: Written expressions of gratitude also play a significant role in personal reflection and growth. The process of writing about gratitude encourages a focus on the positive aspects of life, promoting a more optimistic outlook. Additionally, it fosters mindfulness and encourages a deeper appreciation for the good in one's life.

Cultivating the habit of writing gratitude letters or journals: Cultivating the habit of writing gratitude letters or keeping a gratitude journal can have lasting benefits. Regularly reflecting on and writing about things one is grateful for can enhance positivity, happiness, and satisfaction. It can also foster a deeper appreciation for life and enhance the quality of relationships.

The Etiquette of Gratitude

The significance of gratitude etiquette in different cultures: Gratitude etiquette varies significantly across different cultures, reflecting differing values, traditions, and social norms. Understanding these cultural nuances is important, as the way gratitude is expressed and received can greatly influence social interactions and relationships. For example, in some cultures, expressing gratitude may be more indirect or understated, while in others, direct expressions of thanks are expected and appreciated.

How understanding gratitude etiquette can improve communication: Understanding gratitude etiquette can greatly improve communication. It can ensure that expressions of gratitude are received in the intended spirit and help avoid misunderstandings. Moreover, understanding the appropriate way to express gratitude in different contexts can promote more effective and respectful communication.

Gratitude: A tool for showing respect and consideration to others: Gratitude is a powerful tool for showing respect and consideration to others. When expressed appropriately, it acknowledges the efforts and kindness of others and shows appreciation for their contribution. This can foster a sense of respect and mutual appreciation, strengthening relationships and promoting positive social interactions.

The role of etiquette in expressing gratitude effectively: Etiquette plays a key role in expressing gratitude effectively. Appropriate gratitude etiquette can ensure that your appreciation is communicated clearly and received positively. It can also help to avoid potential social awkwardness or misunderstandings that may arise from culturally inappropriate or misunderstood expressions of thanks.

Cultivating an understanding of gratitude etiquette in various contexts: Cultivating an understanding of gratitude etiquette involves learning and adapting to the norms and expectations in various social and cultural contexts. This might involve researching cultural norms, observing and learning from others, and being open and adaptable in different social situations. Over time, this understanding can help to navigate social interactions more effectively, fostering positive and respectful relationships.

Gratitude and Spirituality: Exploring the Connection Between Gratitude and Inner Growth

M*any spiritual traditions, from Christianity to Buddhism, regard gratitude as a pivotal component of spiritual development.*

Gratitude in Different Spiritual Traditions

The role of gratitude in various religious and spiritual traditions: Gratitude plays a central role in many religious and spiritual traditions. In Christianity, for instance, the act of giving thanks is a recurring theme in the Bible. In Buddhism, gratitude is regarded as a fundamental virtue that cultivates generosity and compassion. In Islam, gratitude to Allah is an essential part of a Muslim's daily life and prayers.

How gratitude is expressed in different cultures and religions: The expressions of gratitude can greatly vary among different cultures and religions. For some, gratitude is expressed through prayer, for others through offerings or sacrifices, and for still others through acts of service. For example, in Hinduism, the ritual of 'Prasad' involves offering food to the deity as a sign of gratitude.

Gratitude: A universal spiritual practice: Despite the differences in how gratitude is expressed, it remains a universal spiritual practice that transcends individual cultures and religions. It's a shared human experience that fosters a sense of connection, humility, and acknowledgment of the blessings and kindness received.

The role of gratitude in spiritual rituals and ceremonies: Gratitude often plays a central role in spiritual rituals and ceremonies. These could range from thanksgiving prayers in Christian worship, offering of alms in Buddhism, to the Islamic prayers of 'Shukr' expressing thanks to God. These rituals serve to regularly remind followers of the importance of gratitude in their spiritual journey.

Cultivating a deeper understanding of gratitude through spiritual traditions: Engaging with spiritual traditions can help cultivate a deeper understanding of gratitude. By learning how gratitude is perceived and practiced in different spiritual contexts, individuals can gain new perspectives and insights, enriching their personal practice of gratitude.

The Role of Gratitude in Spiritual Awakening and Personal Transformation

The transformative power of gratitude in spiritual growth: Gratitude can be a powerful catalyst for spiritual growth. By fostering a mindset of appreciation, individuals can shift their focus from lack to abundance, from fear to love, and from self-centeredness to compassion. This transformation in perspective can spur personal growth and deepen one's spiritual journey.

How gratitude can lead to a deeper sense of purpose and meaning: Gratitude can help individuals find a deeper sense of purpose and meaning in life. By acknowledging the gifts and blessings in their lives, individuals can develop a heightened sense of interconnectedness and a deeper appreciation for life's experiences. This can lead to a more profound understanding of one's purpose and a greater sense of fulfillment.

Gratitude: A catalyst for spiritual awakening: Gratitude can serve as a catalyst for spiritual awakening. The practice of gratitude can help individuals become more present and aware, fostering a deeper connection with their inner self and the world around them. This heightened state of consciousness and connectedness can facilitate spiritual awakening.

The role of gratitude in enhancing spiritual well-being: Gratitude plays a significant role in enhancing spiritual well-being. It helps cultivate a positive mindset, fosters a sense of peace and contentment, and nurtures a deeper connection with the divine or the universe. These factors can greatly enhance an individual's spiritual well-being and overall quality of life.

Cultivating spiritual growth through gratitude: Cultivating spiritual growth through gratitude involves integrating gratitude practices into daily life.

This could involve keeping a gratitude journal, expressing thanks in prayers or meditations, or consciously acknowledging and appreciating life's blessings. Over time, these practices can facilitate spiritual growth and transformation.

Gratitude and Mindfulness

The connection between gratitude and mindfulness: Gratitude and mindfulness are deeply interconnected. Mindfulness, which involves being fully present and engaged in the current moment, enables us to notice and appreciate the good things in our lives. On the other hand, practicing gratitude can increase mindfulness by making us more aware of our blessings, leading to a greater appreciation of the present moment.

How gratitude can foster a greater sense of presence and awareness: When we express gratitude, we take the time to notice, acknowledge, and appreciate the good things in our lives. This act of recognizing our blessings brings us back to the present moment and enhances our awareness of our surroundings and experiences, thereby fostering a greater sense of presence.

Gratitude: A key component of mindful living: Gratitude is a crucial part of living mindfully. By regularly expressing gratitude, we shift our focus from what we lack to what we have, from negative experiences to positive ones. This shift in perspective promotes a positive mindset, reduces stress, and enhances our overall well-being, all of which are key aspects of mindful living.

The role of gratitude in mindfulness-based practices: In mindfulness-based practices, such as mindfulness-based stress reduction (MBSR) or mindfulness-based cognitive therapy (MBCT), gratitude can serve as a valuable tool for grounding one's awareness in the present moment. By focusing on our blessings, we can anchor our attention and cultivate a more peaceful and balanced state of mind.

Cultivating mindfulness through gratitude: To cultivate mindfulness through gratitude, one can start by keeping a gratitude journal, expressing thanks daily, or simply taking a moment to acknowledge one's blessings. These practices can help to enhance mindfulness by fostering a greater awareness and appreciation of the present moment.

The Sacredness of Gratitude

The sacred aspect of gratitude in spiritual traditions: In many spiritual traditions, gratitude is considered a sacred practice. It's seen as a way of acknowledging the divine or the sacred in one's life. For example, in Christianity, expressions of gratitude in prayers and hymns are a way of acknowledging God's blessings. In Buddhism, expressions of gratitude towards others are seen as a form of recognizing the interconnectedness of all beings.

How gratitude can help us recognize the divine in everyday life: By focusing on our blessings and expressing gratitude, we can start to see the divine or the sacred in everyday life. The act of expressing gratitude can make us more aware of the beauty, kindness, and love that surround us, which can be seen as manifestations of the divine.

Gratitude: A path to experiencing the sacred: Expressing gratitude can be a path to experiencing the sacred. By acknowledging and appreciating the good in our lives, we can shift our perspective to see the world as a gift, fostering a deeper connection to the sacred or the divine.

The role of gratitude in deepening our spiritual connection: Gratitude can play a key role in deepening our spiritual connection. By expressing gratitude, we acknowledge our blessings and express our appreciation to the divine or the universe. This practice can foster a sense of humility, interconnectedness, and a deeper spiritual connection.

Cultivating a sense of the sacred through gratitude: To cultivate a sense of the sacred through gratitude, one can integrate gratitude practices into daily spiritual or mindfulness practices. This could involve expressing gratitude in prayers or meditations, keeping a gratitude journal, or simply taking a moment each day to appreciate the beauty and blessings in one's life. These practices can help to cultivate a sense of the sacred and deepen one's spiritual connection.

Gratitude as a Spiritual Practice

The practice of gratitude in various spiritual disciplines: Gratitude plays a central role in many spiritual disciplines. In Christianity, for instance, believers are encouraged to express gratitude to God through prayers and hymns. In Buddhism, gratitude is a way of acknowledging the interconnectedness of all beings and the gifts of life. Sufism, a mystical branch of Islam, considers gratitude as a path to recognizing the divine in all aspects of life. Even in non-religious spiritual practices, gratitude is often considered a path to personal growth and self-discovery.

How integrating gratitude into your spiritual practice can enhance spiritual growth: Incorporating gratitude into your spiritual routine can greatly enhance your spiritual growth. When we express gratitude, we shift our focus from our troubles to our blessings. This positive focus can help us to connect more deeply with the divine or the universe, increase our understanding of ourselves and our place in the world, and foster a more positive, peaceful mindset - all of which are key components of spiritual growth.

Gratitude: A spiritual practice for daily life: Gratitude can be a simple yet powerful spiritual practice that can be easily incorporated into daily life. Whether it's taking a moment to appreciate the beauty of nature, expressing thanks for a kind gesture, or acknowledging the blessing of a new day, these small acts of gratitude can help us to stay connected to the divine in our everyday lives, fostering a deeper sense of spiritual connection and well-being.

The role of gratitude in nurturing a spiritual lifestyle: Gratitude plays a crucial role in nurturing a spiritual lifestyle. By regularly expressing gratitude, we cultivate a positive mindset that enables us to appreciate life's blessings and see the divine in everyday experiences. This can result in a greater sense of peace, purpose, and connection to the divine, all of which are key elements of a spiritual lifestyle.

Cultivating a regular gratitude practice as part of your spiritual journey: Cultivating a regular gratitude practice can be a transformative part of your spiritual journey. This could involve keeping a gratitude journal, where you write down things you're grateful for each day, or integrating expressions of gratitude into your daily prayers or meditations. Regularly practicing gratitude can help you to cultivate a deeper sense of spirituality, fostering a closer connection to the divine and promoting personal growth and transformation.

A Grateful Worldview: Embracing the Beauty of Life's Imperfections

*"*P*erfect is the enemy of good." - Voltaire*

Gratitude and Impermanence

The role of gratitude in embracing life's impermanence: Gratitude can play a key role in helping us accept and embrace the impermanence of life. By appreciating what we have in the present moment, we can learn to cherish it while acknowledging its transient nature. This can lead to a deeper appreciation of life and a greater capacity to embrace change.

How gratitude can help us appreciate the transient nature of life: Gratitude encourages us to focus on the present moment and appreciate what we have right now. This act of appreciation can help us to recognize and accept the transient nature of life. By being grateful, we are acknowledging that our experiences, both good and bad, are temporary, which can help us appreciate our life as it is right now.

Gratitude: A tool for cultivating acceptance of change and impermanence: Gratitude can help us to cultivate acceptance of life's inevitable changes and impermanence. By expressing gratitude for our experiences, we acknowledge their value in the present moment, making it easier to let go when the time comes. This acceptance can lead to a sense of peace and tranquility, even in the face of life's constant changes.

The role of gratitude in dealing with loss and change: Gratitude can be an effective tool in dealing with loss and change. Even in difficult times, finding aspects of our life to be grateful for can provide comfort and perspective, helping us to navigate through loss and change with greater resilience and acceptance.

Cultivating an attitude of gratitude amidst life's impermanence: Cultivating an attitude of gratitude can provide a counterbalance to the challenges posed by life's impermanence. By focusing on what we are grateful for, we shift our perspective from loss and change to appreciation and acceptance, helping us to navigate life's ups and downs with greater equanimity.

Finding Beauty in the Mundane

The role of gratitude in finding beauty in everyday life: Gratitude plays a crucial role in helping us find beauty in everyday life. By practicing gratitude, we train ourselves to look for the good in every situation, to appreciate the little things that often go unnoticed. This can transform our perspective and allow us to find beauty in the most ordinary moments.

How gratitude can help us appreciate ordinary moments: Gratitude encourages us to slow down and pay attention to the ordinary moments that make up our day. By expressing gratitude for these moments, we learn to appreciate them more fully, recognizing the joy, beauty, and lessons they provide.

Gratitude: A tool for celebrating everyday miracles: Gratitude can help us to recognize and celebrate the everyday miracles in our lives - a beautiful sunset, a delicious meal, a moment of connection with a loved one. By taking the time to express gratitude for these experiences, we can transform our perception and experience of our day-to-day life.

The role of gratitude in transforming mundane experiences into moments of joy: Gratitude has the power to transform mundane experiences into moments of joy. By choosing to focus on and appreciate the positive aspects of our daily experiences, we can find joy and beauty in the simplest things, such as a warm cup of coffee, a smile from a stranger, or a comfortable bed at the end of the day.

Cultivating a sense of wonder and appreciation for the mundane through gratitude: Cultivating a sense of wonder and appreciation for the mundane is a natural outcome of practicing gratitude. As we make it a habit to express gratitude for our everyday experiences, we begin to see them in a new light. This shift in perspective can fill our lives with a sense of wonder, making even the most ordinary moments extraordinary, gratitude-worthy moments.

Gratitude for Nature

The role of gratitude in deepening our connection to nature: Gratitude can play a key role in deepening our connection with nature. By expressing gratitude for the natural world, we acknowledge its intrinsic value and importance to our well-being. This act of appreciation can foster a deeper connection with nature, encouraging us to take the time to truly engage with the environment around us.

How expressing gratitude for nature can enhance well-being and environmental awareness: Expressing gratitude for nature can have a profound impact on our well-being and environmental awareness. By appreciating the beauty and benefits of the natural world, we can experience greater joy and tranquility. Additionally, this gratitude can increase our awareness of the environment, motivating us to take action to protect and preserve it.

Gratitude: A path to a deeper appreciation of the natural world: Gratitude is a powerful tool for deepening our appreciation of the natural world. By regularly expressing gratitude for nature, we train ourselves to notice and appreciate the beauty and complexity of the environment, leading to a greater sense of wonder and respect for the natural world.

The role of gratitude in fostering sustainable living practices: Gratitude can also play a role in fostering sustainable living practices. When we're grateful for the natural world, we're more likely to value it and to make choices that reflect this value. This can lead to more sustainable lifestyle choices, such as reducing waste, conserving resources, and supporting environmentally friendly practices.

Cultivating a deeper appreciation for nature through gratitude: We can cultivate a deeper appreciation for nature by integrating gratitude into our interactions with the natural world. This could be as simple as expressing thanks for a beautiful sunset, appreciating the sound of birdsong, or acknowledging the comfort of a cool breeze on a hot day. Over time, this practice of gratitude can lead to a profound appreciation for the beauty and complexity of nature.

Embracing Uncertainty

The role of gratitude in coping with uncertainty and change: Gratitude can play a significant role in helping us cope with uncertainty and change. By expressing gratitude, we can shift our focus from what is uncertain or changing to what is stable and positive in our lives. This shift in perspective can provide comfort and stability in uncertain times.

How gratitude can foster resilience and adaptability in the face of uncertainty: Gratitude can foster resilience and adaptability in the face of uncertainty by helping us to focus on the positive aspects of our lives, even when faced with challenges or change. This positive focus can give us the strength and flexibility to adapt to new circumstances, fostering resilience in the face of uncertainty.

Gratitude: A tool for cultivating peace amidst uncertainty: Gratitude can be a powerful tool for cultivating peace amidst uncertainty. By helping us to focus on what we have rather than what we lack, gratitude can foster a sense of contentment and peace, even in the face of uncertainty.

The role of gratitude in managing life's unexpected challenges: Gratitude can also play a significant role in managing life's unexpected challenges. By helping us to focus on the positive aspects of our lives and to appreciate what we have, gratitude can provide a sense of stability and optimism that can help us navigate through life's unexpected challenges.

Gratitude for Life's Lessons

The role of gratitude in learning from life's challenges and growth opportunities: Gratitude plays an essential role in learning from life's challenges and growth opportunities. When we are grateful, we shift our perspective from seeing difficulties as insurmountable obstacles to viewing them as opportunities for growth and learning. This shift in perspective enables us to embrace challenges with a positive attitude, facilitating personal development and resilience.

How gratitude can transform difficult experiences into valuable lessons: By adopting a mindset of gratitude, we can transform difficult experiences into valuable lessons. When we express gratitude, we acknowledge the good that exists even in the toughest situations. This doesn't mean ignoring or minimizing the pain and difficulty, but rather recognizing that challenging experiences can often provide us with insights, wisdom, and strength that we wouldn't have gained otherwise.

Gratitude: A tool for cultivating a growth mindset: Gratitude is a powerful tool for cultivating a growth mindset. By expressing gratitude for our challenges and the lessons they bring, we embrace the idea that we can learn and grow from our experiences. This attitude is at the heart of a growth mindset, the belief that our abilities and intelligence can be developed over time through dedication and hard work.

The role of gratitude in fostering resilience and personal growth: Gratitude also plays a significant role in fostering resilience and personal growth. When we appreciate the lessons life offers us, even when they're wrapped in difficulties, we build resilience, as we are training ourselves to recover and grow from challenging situations. This resilience leads to personal growth, as we learn to navigate life's ups and downs with grace and tenacity.

Cultivating an appreciation for life's lessons through gratitude: Cultivating an appreciation for life's lessons involves consciously acknowledging and expressing gratitude for the growth opportunities life presents us, even when they come in the form of challenges or difficulties. This can be done through practices like journaling, mindfulness, or simply taking a moment each day to reflect on what we've learned. By consistently practicing gratitude, we can cultivate a deeper appreciation for the lessons life offers us.

Gratitude in Difficult Times: Cultivating Resilience and Hope

"In *life's harshest moments, gratitude illuminates the shadows, reminding us there's still light to be found."*

Gratitude Amidst Personal Challenges

The role of gratitude in navigating personal adversity: Gratitude can play a vital role in navigating personal adversity by providing a perspective shift. When we focus on the things we're grateful for, it can help to diminish the overwhelming negative emotions that often accompany adversity. It doesn't eliminate the problem, but it can make it more manageable by reminding us of the positive aspects of our lives.

How gratitude can provide solace and strength during difficult times: Gratitude, by its nature, is uplifting and can provide comfort and strength during challenging times. It allows us to acknowledge the good in our lives, which can be a source of solace when faced with hardships. Furthermore, when we express gratitude, it often results in feelings of connectedness with others, which can provide additional strength to cope with difficulties.

Gratitude: A tool for maintaining hope and positivity amidst challenges: Expressing gratitude helps us focus on what's going well in our lives, which can boost our optimism and foster hope for the future. This positive focus can help us maintain resilience and a positive outlook, even when faced with significant challenges.

The role of gratitude in personal healing and recovery: Gratitude can play a significant role in personal healing and recovery by shifting our focus from what is wrong to what is right in our lives. This shift can help to reduce stress, increase feelings of well-being, and facilitate psychological healing and recovery.

Cultivating resilience through gratitude during personal challenges: Building a gratitude practice can enhance our resilience during personal challenges. By routinely acknowledging what we are grateful for, we can better weather hardships and bounce back from adversity. This might involve keeping a gratitude journal, praying, meditating, or simply taking a moment each day to mentally list things you appreciate.

Gratitude in Times of Loss and Grief

The role of gratitude in coping with loss and grief: Gratitude can play a significant role in coping with loss and grief. By focusing on the positive memories and experiences we had with the person we've lost, we can start to shift our feelings from deep sorrow to appreciation. This shift is not about ignoring the pain but about acknowledging and cherishing the good times, which can be a crucial part of the healing process.

How gratitude can aid in the grieving process and foster healing: Gratitude can foster healing by helping us focus on the love and positive experiences that remain, even in the face of loss. It can help us see beyond our pain and recognize the gifts that our loved ones have left us, whether these are lessons, memories, or ongoing influences in our lives.

Gratitude: A tool for finding hope amidst sorrow: Expressing gratitude, even in the midst of grief, can help us find hope. It can remind us that even though we've suffered a loss, there are still things in our lives to appreciate and look forward to. This sense of hope can be an essential component in navigating the grieving process.

The role of gratitude in cherishing memories and honoring lost loved ones: Gratitude allows us to cherish the memories of our loved ones and honor their influence in our lives. By expressing thankfulness for the time and experiences shared, we keep their memory alive and acknowledge their ongoing presence in our hearts and minds.

Cultivating gratitude amidst grief to support healing and acceptance: Cultivating gratitude during grief involves consciously acknowledging and giving thanks for the positive impacts our loved ones had on our lives. Regularly expressing gratitude can help us accept our loss over time, supporting our healing journey. It's important to note, however, that everyone's grief process is unique, and this approach may not feel appropriate for every situation.

Gratitude and Mental Health Challenges

The role of gratitude in managing mental health challenges: Gratitude has been found to have various mental health benefits, including reduced symptoms of depression and anxiety. By focusing on what is good in life, gratitude can help shift the mind away from negative thought patterns that can exacerbate mental health challenges.

How gratitude can enhance well-being and resilience in individuals with mental health issues: Regular practice of gratitude can help individuals develop a more positive outlook, which in turn can boost overall well-being and resilience. It can help buffer against stress and negativity, which are often heightened in individuals with mental health issues.

Gratitude: A tool for fostering self-compassion and self-care in mental health: Gratitude not only helps us appreciate others but can also be turned inward to foster self-compassion. By being thankful for our strengths and forgiving our weaknesses, gratitude can promote self-care, a crucial aspect of managing mental health.

The role of gratitude in therapeutic practices for mental health: Many therapists incorporate gratitude exercises into their practices, such as keeping a gratitude journal or consciously reflecting on things to be grateful for. These exercises can help shift focus away from distressing thoughts and promote a more balanced perspective.

Cultivating gratitude as part of a holistic approach to mental health care: Gratitude can be part of a comprehensive approach to mental health care. In combination with therapies like cognitive-behavioral therapy (CBT), medication, mindfulness, and self-care practices, gratitude can contribute to improved mental health outcomes.

Gratitude in Times of Global Crisis

The role of gratitude in navigating global crises and upheaval: In times of global crisis, gratitude can serve as a grounding practice that helps individuals maintain perspective, even amidst widespread uncertainty and fear. By focusing on what we are grateful for, we can better manage stress and anxiety.

How collective gratitude can foster unity, resilience, and hope in times of crisis: Collective expressions of gratitude can help foster a sense of unity and shared humanity. This can contribute to resilience by encouraging mutual support and cooperation, while also fostering hope for a better future.

Gratitude: A tool for maintaining perspective and positivity in challenging times: When faced with a global crisis, it's easy to get overwhelmed by negative news and fear. Gratitude can serve as a tool to help maintain perspective, focus on the positive, and reinforce our ability to cope.

The role of gratitude in community resilience and recovery in the aftermath of a crisis: After a crisis, gratitude can play a role in recovery and resilience at the community level. Expressions of gratitude for support received, for example, can strengthen community bonds and contribute to collective healing.

Cultivating a culture of gratitude to promote collective healing and hope: Cultivating a culture of gratitude involves promoting and valuing expressions of thankfulness at the community or societal level. Such a culture can contribute to collective healing after a crisis by reinforcing positivity, unity, and hope.

Gratitude for Life's Unwanted Gifts

The role of gratitude in appreciating life's unwanted gifts or lessons: Life often presents us with challenges and difficulties that, at first glance, don't seem like gifts at all. However, these "unwanted gifts" often come with hidden lessons or growth opportunities. Gratitude can help us shift our perspective to appreciate these lessons and growth opportunities.

How gratitude can transform our perception of challenges and hardships: Practicing gratitude in the face of adversity can transform our perception of challenges. Instead of seeing hardships as insurmountable obstacles, we can begin to view them as opportunities for growth and learning. This shift in perspective can make the experience of hardship more manageable and even beneficial.

Gratitude: A tool for recognizing the hidden blessings in difficult situations: Every challenge comes with its silver lining, but it can often be difficult to see it in the midst of hardship. Gratitude can act as a tool to uncover these hidden blessings, helping us to recognize the good that can come from difficult situations.

The role of gratitude in fostering personal growth and resilience: Gratitude not only helps us appreciate the good in life but also makes us more resilient in the face of adversity. By being thankful for life's challenges and the lessons they bring, we can build inner strength and adaptability, which are key components of resilience.

Cultivating gratitude for life's unwanted gifts as part of a resilient mindset: Incorporating gratitude into our daily routine, especially in times of hardship, can help cultivate a resilient mindset. This involves consciously acknowledging and appreciating the lessons and growth opportunities that come with life's unwanted gifts. Over time, this practice can make us more resilient and better equipped to handle future challenges.

Gratitude and Aging: Embracing the Golden Years with Grace and Appreciation

"Every passing year brings with it a thousand moments to be grateful for."

The Role of Gratitude in Healthy Aging

The importance of gratitude in promoting emotional and physical well-being in older adults: Gratitude can have significant benefits for the emotional and physical well-being of older adults. Emotionally, it helps promote a positive mood, reduce stress, and increase life satisfaction. Physically, the positivity derived from gratitude can contribute to better sleep, less fatigue, and potentially lower levels of inflammation.

How gratitude can enhance life satisfaction and positivity in the golden years: As individuals age, they may face several changes including health issues, loss of loved ones, or retirement. Gratitude can help in maintaining a positive outlook amidst these changes, enhancing life satisfaction by encouraging a focus on the blessings and positive experiences in life, rather than losses or regrets.

Gratitude: A tool for embracing aging with grace and acceptance: Gratitude can help older adults accept the aging process with grace. By focusing on the positive aspects of aging, such as wisdom, experience, and personal growth, gratitude can shift the perspective on aging from one of loss to one of gain.

The role of gratitude in promoting resilience and adaptability in older adults: Gratitude can foster resilience in older adults by helping them navigate life's challenges with a positive mindset. By appreciating life's ups and downs, they can develop a greater capacity to adapt to change, which is crucial in later life.

Cultivating a gratitude practice to support healthy aging: A regular gratitude practice, such as keeping a gratitude journal or expressing thanks daily, can support emotional and physical health in older adults. These practices can also foster a positive attitude towards aging and enhance overall life satisfaction.

Gratitude and Legacy

The role of gratitude in reflecting on one's legacy and life's accomplishments: As individuals reflect on their life's journey, gratitude allows them to recognize and appreciate their achievements and the impact they've made. This can bring a sense of fulfillment and pride in one's legacy.

How gratitude can foster a sense of fulfillment and purpose in older adults: Gratitude can contribute to a sense of life purpose for older adults by allowing them to appreciate their life's journey and the contributions they have made. This can provide a sense of fulfillment and a positive self-concept in later life.

Gratitude: A tool for honoring one's life journey and experiences: Gratitude allows individuals to honor their life's experiences, both good and bad, by recognizing how these experiences have contributed to their growth and shaped their legacy.

The role of gratitude in legacy planning and end-of-life conversations: Gratitude can play a significant role in legacy planning and end-of-life conversations. By focusing on what they are grateful for, individuals can express what is most important to them, helping to shape discussions around their values, wishes, and the legacy they wish to leave.

Cultivating gratitude for life's journey as part of a meaningful legacy: Cultivating a sense of gratitude for one's life journey and experiences can be a profound way to reflect on and shape one's legacy. A regular gratitude practice can help individuals recognize the value of their life's experiences and the impact they have had, contributing to a meaningful and lasting legacy.

Gratitude in Coping with Age-Related Challenges

The role of gratitude in managing age-related challenges and transitions: Ageing often comes with numerous changes and transitions such as retirement, changes in health status, or loss of loved ones. Gratitude can help manage these transitions by focusing on the positives in life, encouraging resilience, and promoting a sense of acceptance.

How gratitude can foster resilience and hope in the face of health challenges or loss: By focusing on the aspects of life one is thankful for, gratitude can help to counterbalance the natural tendency to focus on problems or losses. This can foster resilience and hope, even in the face of health challenges or the loss of loved ones.

Gratitude: A tool for maintaining positivity and acceptance amidst aging: By focusing on the blessings and positive experiences in life, gratitude can help maintain a positive outlook and promote acceptance of the aging process.

The role of gratitude in supporting a healthy aging process, even in the face of difficulties: Gratitude can help individuals see beyond their difficulties, appreciate their strengths and capabilities, and recognize the support they have around them. This positivity can contribute to a healthier aging process.

Cultivating gratitude as a coping mechanism for age-related challenges: Regularly practicing gratitude, such as through a gratitude journal or expressing thanks to others, can be an effective coping mechanism for managing age-related challenges. This practice can foster resilience, promote a positive mindset, and improve overall well-being.

Gratitude for the Wisdom of Age

The role of gratitude in appreciating the wisdom and perspective that come with age: Gratitude can help individuals appreciate the wisdom and perspective that come with age. It encourages a focus on the valuable life lessons learned, the growth experienced, and the maturity gained over the years.

How gratitude can foster a sense of pride and appreciation for one's accumulated wisdom: Gratitude allows individuals to acknowledge and appreciate their life experiences and the wisdom gained from them. This can foster a sense of pride and self-worth.

Gratitude: A tool for celebrating the knowledge and experience that come with age: Gratitude can help people celebrate the knowledge, insights, and experiences that come with age, viewing them as precious resources rather than signs of decline.

The role of gratitude in fostering intergenerational connections: Gratitude for the wisdom of age can foster stronger intergenerational connections. By expressing gratitude for the wisdom and experiences of older adults, younger generations can gain valuable insights and perspectives, promoting mutual respect and understanding.

The role of gratitude in recognizing the value and contribution of elders: Gratitude can play a vital role in recognizing and appreciating the value and contributions of elders in our societies. This can promote respect and dignity for older adults, acknowledging their integral role in the community.

Cultivating gratitude for the wisdom of age in our societies: Cultivating gratitude for the wisdom of age involves recognizing and appreciating the unique insights, perspectives, and experiences that older adults bring to our communities. It encourages a societal shift in how we view and value aging, promoting respect and appreciation for the wisdom of age.

Gratitude Practices for Seniors

The importance of cultivating gratitude practices tailored for seniors: The physiological and emotional changes that accompany aging can sometimes lead to feelings of discontent or unhappiness. Gratitude practices tailored for seniors can help them focus on the positive aspects of their lives, fostering resilience, enhancing their emotional well-being, and promoting a more optimistic outlook on life. Tailored practices can account for unique aspects of seniors' lives, such as mobility limitations or health issues, making the practice more accessible and beneficial.

How gratitude practices can enhance the quality of life for seniors: Gratitude practices can lead to various positive outcomes such as improved mood, better sleep, reduced feelings of loneliness and isolation, and enhanced overall well-being. They can foster a greater appreciation for life, deepen relationships, and provide a sense of purpose and fulfillment, thereby enhancing the quality of life for seniors.

Gratitude: A tool for promoting mental agility and emotional well-being in seniors: Regular gratitude practice encourages the brain to consistently focus on positive thoughts and experiences, which can enhance mental agility by promoting cognitive flexibility. Moreover, by shifting focus away from negative emotions, gratitude can enhance emotional well-being and stability, potentially mitigating symptoms of depression and anxiety.

The role of gratitude practices in senior care and wellness programs: Incorporating gratitude practices into senior care and wellness programs can contribute to a holistic approach to senior health. These practices can be a non-pharmaceutical intervention to improve mental health, enhance social connections, and promote overall well-being. Activities might include gratitude journaling, sharing gratitude in group settings, creating gratitude art, or expressing thanks to loved ones.

Cultivating effective and meaningful gratitude practices for seniors: Cultivating effective gratitude practices for seniors involves understanding their unique circumstances, preferences, and abilities. For some, a daily gratitude journal might be beneficial, while others might prefer sharing what they're grateful for with a friend or family member. Others might find gratitude in quiet reflection or prayer. The key is to make the practice accessible and enjoyable, encouraging regular engagement. Incorporating gratitude into everyday activities or rituals can also make the practice more meaningful and sustainable. For instance, expressing gratitude over meals, during morning routines, or before bedtime can help to cultivate a consistent gratitude practice.

Living a Life of Gratitude: Embodying Gratitude in Daily Life

*E*mbarking on this journey isn't just about saying 'thank you.' It's *about transforming your view of the world, one moment of appreciation at a time.*

Cultivating a Daily Gratitude Practice

The importance of integrating gratitude into your daily routine: Integrating gratitude into your daily routine is a powerful practice that can significantly influence your perspective and overall mood. Regularly focusing on what you are thankful for helps shift your attention away from negative aspects and challenges, allowing you to appreciate life's simple pleasures and joys. This practice of regular appreciation can enhance mental health, improve relationships, and cultivate a more positive outlook on life.

How a daily gratitude practice can transform your outlook and well-being: A daily gratitude practice helps to rewire the brain to focus more on positive aspects of life, thereby reducing the mental space occupied by negative thoughts and experiences. Over time, this can enhance your psychological well-being, improving mood, reducing stress, and fostering overall happiness. Moreover, gratitude has been linked to physical health benefits, including improved sleep and a healthier heart, contributing to an overall sense of well-being.

Gratitude: A tool for mindfulness and presence in daily life: Practicing gratitude encourages mindfulness - a focused awareness on the present moment. By appreciating what you have in the here and now, you can become more attuned to your present circumstances, rather than worrying about the past or future. This can help reduce anxiety, increase contentment, and foster a deeper connection with yourself and others.

The role of daily gratitude practices in fostering sustained positivity: Regular gratitude practices help sustain a positive attitude by consistently drawing your focus to the good in your life. Even on difficult days, recognizing small things to be grateful for can provide a sense of positivity. This can build emotional resilience over time, helping you to maintain a positive attitude through ups and downs.

Cultivating a consistent and impactful daily gratitude practice: Developing a consistent gratitude practice involves setting aside a specific time each day to reflect on what you're thankful for. This could be done through various methods such as keeping a gratitude journal, saying a mental or out-loud thank you for the good in your life, or meditating on your blessings. The most impactful gratitude practices are personal and meaningful to you. It's also helpful to include why you're grateful for each item, as this deepens the emotional impact of the practice.

Gratitude in Relationships

The role of gratitude in nurturing and enhancing relationships: Gratitude plays a crucial role in relationships by helping to build and maintain mutual appreciation and respect. Expressing gratitude for your partner's actions, for instance, makes them feel valued and acknowledged, which strengthens the bond between you. Additionally, gratitude can help counteract negative interactions, helping relationships to survive and thrive through difficult times.

How expressing gratitude can foster deeper connections and understanding in relationships: Expressing gratitude towards others can lead to deeper connections as it shows that you acknowledge and value their contributions to your life. This can improve communication, increase trust, and encourage a greater understanding between individuals. It makes people feel seen and appreciated, deepening the emotional bond between them.

Gratitude: A tool for appreciation and positivity in interactions with others: By focusing on the positive aspects of your relationships and expressing gratitude for them, you can foster more positive interactions with others.

Gratitude can help to balance out any negative aspects or conflicts and create a more appreciative and understanding atmosphere in your relationships.

The role of gratitude in conflict resolution and relationship building: Gratitude can play a significant role in conflict resolution by shifting focus away from blame and towards appreciation. Recognizing the positive aspects of your relationship even in times of disagreement can help to de-escalate conflicts, facilitate compromise, and promote mutual understanding. Furthermore, expressing gratitude after a conflict can aid in healing and rebuilding the relationship, providing a stronger foundation for future interactions.

Cultivating gratitude in relationships for mutual growth and happiness: To cultivate gratitude in relationships, it's important to consciously recognize and express appreciation for the other person's actions and qualities. This can be done verbally or through actions, such as writing a thank-you note, spending quality time together, or doing something special for them. Regularly practicing gratitude in this way can foster mutual growth, as both individuals feel appreciated and valued, leading to increased satisfaction and happiness in the relationship. Importantly, gratitude in relationships should be genuine and specific to be most effective. It's not just about saying "thank you," but about communicating sincere appreciation for the unique qualities and actions of the other person.

Gratitude at Work

The role of gratitude in promoting job satisfaction and workplace positivity: Gratitude in the workplace can significantly boost job satisfaction, morale, and overall positivity. When employees feel valued and recognized for their contributions, they are more likely to be content with their job and exhibit a positive attitude. A gratitude-based culture encourages the acknowledgment of each other's efforts and achievements, fostering a sense of camaraderie and positive energy within the team. It's not just about recognizing big wins, but also about appreciating the small contributions that often go unnoticed.

How expressing gratitude can foster a positive work environment and enhance productivity: Expressing gratitude in the workplace can create a more positive, supportive, and collaborative work environment. When employees feel appreciated, they are more likely to be engaged, motivated, and productive. Additionally, gratitude can reduce workplace stress and burnout by promoting a more positive outlook and better coping strategies. For instance, a manager thanking a team member for their hard work on a project can boost that individual's morale, making them feel seen and valued, which can in turn drive increased productivity.

Gratitude: A tool for appreciation and team building in the workplace: Gratitude can be a powerful tool for strengthening team relationships and building a more cohesive work unit. When team members regularly express appreciation for each other's efforts, it can lead to higher levels of trust, cooperation, and mutual respect. Gratitude can also help in reducing workplace conflicts and improving communication, as it fosters a culture of openness, understanding, and recognition of diverse contributions.

The role of gratitude in leadership and employee engagement: Leaders play a crucial role in fostering a culture of gratitude within the workplace. By expressing appreciation for their team's efforts and achievements, leaders can boost employee morale, engagement, and loyalty. Furthermore, leaders who model gratitude show that they value their employees not just as workers, but as individuals, which can promote a deeper level of commitment and motivation among the team. Effective leaders understand that gratitude is not a one-time event, but a continuous practice that helps in building a stronger, more engaged team.

Cultivating a culture of gratitude at work for overall organizational success: To cultivate a culture of gratitude at work, it's important to integrate appreciation into the organization's core values and daily practices. This could include implementing regular recognition programs, encouraging peer-to-peer appreciation, or providing platforms for employees to share their gratitude stories. Research has shown that companies with a strong culture of gratitude often see improved employee satisfaction, lower turnover, and better overall performance. Therefore, cultivating gratitude at work is not just beneficial for individual employees, but also for the overall success of the organization.

Gratitude and Personal Growth

The role of gratitude in fostering personal growth and self-improvement: Gratitude plays a significant role in promoting personal growth and self-improvement. By fostering an appreciation for what we have and where we are in life, gratitude can motivate us to strive for continued growth and development. It can help us shift our focus from what we lack to what we already possess and have achieved, promoting a positive outlook that is conducive to self-improvement.

How gratitude can enhance self-awareness and foster a growth mindset: Gratitude promotes self-awareness by encouraging us to reflect on our blessings, achievements, and experiences. This reflective process allows us to gain a deeper understanding of ourselves, our values, and our desires. Additionally, practicing gratitude can foster a growth mindset. By focusing on what we are thankful for, we are more likely to see challenges as opportunities for learning and growth rather than obstacles.

Gratitude: A tool for appreciation and learning in personal development: Gratitude serves as a powerful tool for appreciating the journey of personal development. It encourages us to value each step we take in our growth, even if it's small or challenging. Through gratitude, we learn to see every experience - good or bad - as an opportunity for learning and growth. This ability to appreciate and learn from all life's experiences is a critical component of personal development.

The role of gratitude in setting and achieving personal goals: Gratitude can play a vital role in goal setting and achievement. By appreciating our past and present, we can gain clarity on what we want for our future. This clarity allows us to set meaningful and fulfilling goals. Furthermore, gratitude encourages us to recognize and celebrate our progress towards our goals, no matter how small. This celebration can boost our motivation and commitment to continue pursuing our goals.

Cultivating gratitude as part of a lifelong journey of personal growth: Gratitude is not just a practice but a lifestyle that supports a lifelong journey of personal growth. By regularly expressing gratitude, we nurture a positive mindset, enhance our self-awareness, and foster a continual desire for growth and improvement. Cultivating gratitude can involve practices like keeping a gratitude journal, expressing thanks to others, and mindfully reflecting on what we appreciate each day. As we incorporate these practices into our lives, we'll find that gratitude becomes an integral part of our journey towards personal growth.

A Lifetime of Gratitude

The role of gratitude in leading a fulfilled and meaningful life: Gratitude plays a pivotal role in leading a fulfilled and meaningful life. By acknowledging the good in our lives and appreciating our experiences - both the highs and the lows - we can find fulfillment and meaning. Gratitude allows us to see value in our everyday experiences and to recognize the interconnectedness of our lives with others, adding a layer of richness and depth to our existence. It also invites a sense of contentment and acceptance that can significantly contribute to our overall fulfillment.

How cultivating a lifelong practice of gratitude can enhance overall life satisfaction: A lifelong practice of gratitude is associated with increased life satisfaction. By regularly acknowledging our blessings and expressing gratitude, we foster positive emotions, improve our relationships, and enhance our overall well-being - all of which contribute to life satisfaction. Furthermore, consistent gratitude practice can help us navigate life's challenges more effectively, boosting our resilience and further enhancing our satisfaction with life.

Gratitude: A tool for maintaining positivity and resilience throughout life's ups and downs: Life is full of ups and downs, and gratitude can serve as a powerful tool for maintaining positivity and resilience amidst these fluctuations. When we face difficulties, gratitude can help shift our focus from what's going wrong to the positives in our life, thus fostering optimism. Moreover, by appreciating our strengths and resources, we can boost our resilience, enabling us to better cope with and bounce back from adversity.

The role of lifelong gratitude in legacy-building and personal fulfillment: Lifelong gratitude can play a significant role in legacy-building and personal fulfillment. As we age, reflecting on our life through the lens of gratitude can help us appreciate our achievements, learn from our experiences, and feel fulfilled. It can also guide us in creating a legacy imbued with gratitude and positivity, impacting future generations. By expressing gratitude for our life journey, we can find fulfillment and contribute to a meaningful legacy.

Cultivating a lifetime of gratitude for lasting happiness and well-being: Cultivating a lifetime of gratitude involves integrating gratitude practices into our daily life, such as expressing thanks, keeping a gratitude journal, or simply taking moments to appreciate the good around us. These practices can significantly enhance our happiness and well-being, leading to a healthier, more positive outlook on life. Moreover, a lifelong gratitude practice can foster resilience, improve relationships, and promote physical health, contributing to our overall well-being for a lifetime.

Conclusion

As we reach the end of this journey through gratitude, it's essential to reflect on the insights and lessons we've learned together. This book has explored the multifaceted nature of gratitude, delving into its science, benefits, and practical applications in various aspects of our lives.

We began by understanding the science behind gratitude and its impact on our physical and emotional well-being. From improving our mental health and relationships to enhancing our resilience in the face of adversity, gratitude has proven to be a powerful force in our lives.

Throughout the book, we discussed various strategies and techniques for cultivating gratitude awareness, such as mindfulness practices, reframing negative thoughts, and building a gratitude routine. We also provided practical tips and activities to help you integrate gratitude into your daily life, including journaling, meditation, and expressing appreciation to others.

Recognizing the challenges that can arise when developing a gratitude practice, we addressed common misconceptions, obstacles, and potential pitfalls. By debunking myths and offering guidance on navigating difficulties, we aimed to create a more balanced and sustainable approach to gratitude.

The book also highlighted the power of gratitude in strengthening relationships, fostering empathy in children, and creating a positive and supportive professional environment. As we explored the role of gratitude in communication, spirituality, and personal growth, we discovered the transformative potential of cultivating a grateful mindset.

In our increasingly interconnected world, the importance of gratitude for our shared humanity and the planet was emphasized. We looked at how gratitude can inspire acts of kindness, community initiatives, and social activism, ultimately contributing to a more compassionate and just world.

Lastly, we provided a roadmap for your gratitude journey, guiding you in assessing your current gratitude baseline, setting goals, and designing a personalized practice that meets your needs. By encouraging self-reflection and accountability, we hope to support you in maintaining a long-term commitment to gratitude and well-being.

As you close this book, remember that gratitude is not a one-time practice or a fleeting emotion. It's a lifelong journey that requires patience, dedication, and self-compassion. We encourage you to continue exploring and deepening your gratitude practice, embracing the beauty of life's imperfections, and cherishing the moments that make life truly extraordinary.

May your heart be filled with gratitude, and may your life be enriched with the countless blessings that come from cultivating a grateful mindset.

A Personal Thank You

D ear Reader,
As we reach the end of this book, I want to take a moment to express my heartfelt gratitude to you. Thank you for embarking on this journey with me, exploring the power of gratitude, and dedicating time and effort to enhance your well-being and the lives of those around you.

Your willingness to delve into the world of gratitude and apply its principles to your life is not only a testament to your personal growth but also a contribution to the betterment of our society. When we cultivate gratitude, we foster a more compassionate, empathetic, and connected world.

I am deeply appreciative of the opportunity to share my passion for gratitude with you. Your support and engagement have inspired and motivated me throughout the writing process. I am humbled by your trust in my work, and I sincerely hope that the insights and practices offered in this book have been valuable to you.

As you continue on your gratitude journey, remember that the road may not always be smooth. There will be challenges, setbacks, and moments of doubt. But know that you are not alone. We are all travelers on this path, striving to cultivate a grateful heart and a life of appreciation.

I encourage you to stay curious, open, and compassionate with yourself and others. Cherish the small victories, learn from the setbacks, and never lose sight of the beauty and wonder that gratitude brings to our lives.

Once again, thank you for joining me on this journey. May your life be enriched with love, joy, and the countless blessings that come from cultivating a grateful heart.

Warmest regards,
Brenda Rebon

Other Books By Brenda Rebon

This book, **"The Gratitude Effect: Transforming Your Life One Thank You At A Time"**, is also available in ebook format.

Another of my popular books, **"101 Positive Affirmations: Positive Inspirational and Motivational Affirmations To Live Your Best Life!"**

Embark on a journey to self-discovery and learn how to embrace your authentic self. Discover the steps you can take to uncover your true passions, purpose, and potential, and how to live a life that is truly in alignment with your values and desires.

Discover how to develop resilience and overcome life's challenges with grace and strength. Learn the strategies and mindset shifts that can help you navigate through difficult times and come out stronger on the other side.

Take your personal development journey to new heights by exploring more of the author's works. Each book is designed to empower you with the tools and insights needed to live your best life. Don't miss the chance to continue your transformative journey with these enlightening reads.

P(101)SITIVE
AFFIRMATIONS

Positive Inspirational and Motivational
Affirmations To Live Your Best Life!

BRENDA REBON

Discover the transformative power of positivity with "**Your Best Year Yet: 365 Daily Positive Inspirational and Motivational Affirmations To Live Your Best Life**" This dynamic book serves as a guide for personal growth, self-improvement, and manifestation, perfect for anyone seeking to embrace change and build a life of abundance.

Are you ready to harness the power of positive thinking? Are you on a journey towards self-discovery, seeking to manifest wealth, love, happiness, and improved health in your life? This remarkable book provides a holistic approach to personal development, combining the power of positive affirmations with actionable strategies that create real change. It's your roadmap to manifesting your desires and actualizing your full potential.

With "**Your Best Year Yet: 365 Daily Positive Inspirational and Motivational Affirmations**" you're getting more than just a book - you're unlocking a daily toolkit for transformation. Each day presents a new affirmation, a powerful thought designed to inspire action, rewire your thinking, and shift your focus towards your goals. These carefully curated affirmations serve as seeds of change, nurturing a growth mindset, fostering resilience, and promoting a lifestyle of abundance and well-being.

Imagine waking up each morning to a powerful affirmation, a guiding thought that propels you towards your goals and dreams. Each day becomes a stepping stone towards a more fulfilling life, one filled with vibrant health, unprecedented wealth, boundless love, unwavering confidence, and robust self-esteem. The consistent practice of these affirmations leads to the development of a positivity habit, one that transforms every aspect of your life and paves the way for success.

So, are you ready to invite abundance into your life? Are you prepared to take actionable steps towards your dreams and become the architect of your reality? "**Your Best Year Yet: 365 Daily Positive Inspirational and Motivational Affirmations**" is the tool you need to start this transformative journey. Don't wait another day - embrace the power of positivity now and watch your life transform for the better.

"**Your Best Year Yet: 365 Daily Positive Inspirational and Motivational Affirmations To Live Your Best Life**" is more than a book. It's an investment in your well-being, a companion on your journey towards self-improvement, and a key to unlocking your full potential. Make it part of your daily ritual and start living the life you've always dreamed of today. Get you copy now and embark on a year-long journey towards abundance and self-fulfillment. Start living your best life today!

Your Best Year Yet

365 Daily Positive Inspirational and Motivational Affirmations To Live Your Best Life

BRENDA REBON

Frequently Asked Questions (FAQs)

- **What is gratitude, and why is it important?**

Gratitude is the act of recognizing and appreciating the positive aspects of life, whether they are big or small. It involves acknowledging the goodness in our lives and the sources of that goodness. Gratitude has been scientifically proven to enhance well-being, happiness, and overall life satisfaction, improve physical health, and strengthen relationships.

- **How does gratitude affect our brains?**

Gratitude has been shown to activate the reward and pleasure centers of the brain, releasing feel-good neurotransmitters such as dopamine and serotonin. It also reduces stress hormones like cortisol and helps to regulate emotions, promoting emotional resilience and well-being.

- **Can gratitude help with anxiety and depression?**

Yes, research has shown that practicing gratitude can help reduce symptoms of anxiety and depression by focusing on positive aspects of life and promoting a more optimistic outlook. Gratitude also helps to create new neural pathways in the brain, which can lead to lasting changes in mood and overall mental health.

- **How do I start practicing gratitude?**

There are many ways to start practicing gratitude, including maintaining a gratitude journal, meditating on gratitude, expressing appreciation to others, and engaging in acts of kindness. The key is to find a method that resonates with you and commit to practicing regularly.

- **How long does it take to see the benefits of practicing gratitude?**

The timeline for experiencing the benefits of gratitude can vary from person to person. Some people may notice improvements in their mood and well-being within days or weeks of consistent practice, while others may take longer to see the effects. The key is to be patient and persistent in your practice.

- **Can practicing gratitude improve my relationships?**

Yes, gratitude has been shown to strengthen relationships by fostering deeper connections, increasing empathy, and improving communication. Expressing appreciation to others can also boost their well-being and create a positive feedback loop, enhancing the overall quality of the relationship.

- **How can I teach gratitude to my children?**

You can teach gratitude to your children by modeling gratitude in your own behavior, engaging in age-appropriate gratitude activities, and encouraging them to express appreciation for the people and things in their lives. It's important to be consistent and patient, as cultivating gratitude takes time and practice.

- **What is the difference between gratitude and thankfulness?**

Gratitude is a broader concept that encompasses not only feeling thankful for specific things but also cultivating an overall mindset of appreciation and recognizing the interconnectedness of life. Thankfulness is a specific expression of gratitude, often focused on particular events, people, or things.

- **Can I practice gratitude even during difficult times?**

Absolutely. In fact, practicing gratitude during challenging times can help to build emotional resilience, shift your perspective, and provide a sense of comfort and hope. It's important to recognize that gratitude does not mean ignoring or denying negative emotions, but rather finding appreciation even amid adversity.

- **What are some common misconceptions about gratitude?**

Some common misconceptions about gratitude include the belief that it's only about saying "thank you," that it requires a specific set of circumstances to be practiced, or that it's a form of complacency. In reality, gratitude is a multifaceted practice that can be cultivated in any situation and involves acknowledging both the positive and the negative aspects of life.

- **How can I maintain my gratitude practice over the long term?**

Maintaining a long-term gratitude practice involves setting realistic goals, being consistent, and staying accountable to yourself or others. It's also important to be patient and recognize that cultivating gratitude is an ongoing process that requires time, commitment, and self-compassion.

Visit My Website for More Helpful Information

Dear Reader,

Thank you for taking the time to read this book and explore the power of gratitude. I hope you've found it insightful, practical, and inspiring. As you continue on your journey to cultivate a grateful mindset, I encourage you to stay connected and seek additional resources to support your growth and understanding.

I invite you to visit my website, **AchieveProgress.com**, where you'll find even more helpful information, tips, and resources on gratitude and personal development. The website offers a wealth of content, including:

- Blog articles on various aspects of gratitude and well-being.
- Videos, podcasts, and interviews featuring experts in the field of gratitude research and practice (currently on our roadmap).
- Downloadable worksheets, exercises, and guided meditations to enhance your gratitude practice (currently on our roadmap).
- Information on workshops, webinars, and courses to help deepen your understanding and skills in cultivating gratitude (currently on our roadmap).
- A supportive community where you can connect with like-minded individuals, share your experiences, and learn from others on their gratitude journey (currently on our roadmap).

By visiting **AchieveProgress.com**, you'll gain access to a treasure trove of knowledge, inspiration, and guidance to support you as you integrate gratitude into your life. Plus, you'll be the first to know about any new books, events, or offerings that become available.

So, don't hesitate! Head over to **AchieveProgress.com** today and discover a wealth of resources designed to help you unlock the full potential of gratitude in your life. I look forward to connecting with you and supporting your journey toward a more grateful, joyful, and fulfilling life.

Warm regards,

Brenda Rebon

Milton Keynes UK
Ingram Content Group UK Ltd.
UKHW020951221123
433051UK00021B/1311